A Lady in Paris During 'The Hundred Days', 1815

A Lady in Paris During 'The Hundred Days', 1815

Letters Covering the Period of Napoleon's Escape
from Elba to the Fall of the Capital

Helen Maria Williams

LEONAUR

A Lady in Paris During 'The Hundred Days', 1815
Letters Covering the Period of Napoleon's Escape from Elba to the Fall of the Capital
by Helen Maria Williams

First published under the title
Narrative of the Events Which have Taken Place in France, from the Landing of Napoleon Bonaparte, on the 1st of March, 1815, Till the Restoration of Louis XVIII. With an Account of the Present State of Society and Public Opinion

Leonaur is an imprint of Oakpast Ltd

ISBN: 978-1-78282-425-1 (hardcover)
ISBN: 978-1-78282-426-8 (softcover)

http://www.leonaur.com

Publisher's Notes

Contents

Letters

LETTER 1.

Paris, April, 1815.

My Dear Sir,

If in the list of moral maxims, anything had been left unsaid upon the evil of procrastination, this would be a fit occasion to add something to the stock of luminous observations made on that subject since the beginning of time. But why have you furnished me with a sad example of the truth of these precepts? Why, when the English hastened in multitudes to Paris, have you delayed your journey from week to week, till it can no longer be accomplished?

Although divided from each other by a geographical space of only a few short leagues, at what an immeasurable distance were the two countries which we inhabit separated by the ascendancy of that Implacable Will, which had placed a barrier between the nations more insurmountable than the wall of China! You will easily believe that I saw with pleasure the arrival once more of those groups of travellers who speak my native language, who remind me of the scenes of early life, who conjure up those images of the past which no heart recalls without emotion, and which "*breathe a second spring*."—But amidst those successive crowds, why have I not seen the friend of my youth?

Why have your chariot-wheels tarried, till I can no longer urge you to come, although I believe you would incur no personal clanger by so doing? Our re-installed emperor is extremely mortified at the precipitation with which the English visitors fly from his dominion. It may indeed be observed, that in our paroxysms of political madness in this country, we have usually imagination enough to blend a little variety in our proceedings; and therefore the English having been once detained, was probably the very reason why they had no such measure again to apprehend; since its folly and impolicy had been amply recognised. The English might therefore have applied to themselves the observation made long since, by M. de la Fayette, to the people, when they wanted the oath of the first federation to be repeated; *"Mes amis, le serment n'est pas une arriette, qu'on joue deux fois."*

Fear, however, is very subject to reason amiss; the English have departed, and you will naturally defer your visit till the end of the present dynasty, which to me excludes not the hope of seeing you, perhaps ere long, in Paris. In the mean time I shall trace, as you desire, in a series of letters, the events which are passing before me, and which you will one day give to the public, if you consider my sketches as worthy its attention. I have been often asked by my countrymen of late, why I have so long discontinued to describe the scenes which are passing around me? I have perhaps done wrong, since I may at least pretend to be qualified for the task, inasmuch as it respects a knowledge of the subject;—I who, during my residence in Paris, have witnessed all the successive phases of its revolutions, who have so long marked the list of its remembrances, its calamities, its triumphs, and its crimes!

But the iron hand of despotism has weighed upon my soul, and subdued all intellectual energy. The Chevalier de Boufflers used to call Bonaparte *"le cochemare de l'univers,"* the nightmare of the world; and indeed the idea of the consequences with which those were menaced who ventured to collect forbidden materials for history, was sufficient to chill this sort of courage. We long believed the tyranny of Bonaparte to be confirmed, while now, persuaded that his new usurpation will not be durable, I shall no longer hang my harp upon the willows, and despair of the future.

I shall begin with the second volume of Napoleon's history, or, to use the words of Madame de Staël, of Bonaparte's adventures, leaving the first volume to a future period, or an abler historian. It would indeed be quite impossible for me, in the present agitation of my mind, to *"begin at the beginning."* I partake the common feeling experienced by all who have witnessed the French Revolution, that of an insuperable repugnance to returning on the past. When we reflect on all we have seen and suffered in this country, the soul recoils from such a host of fearful recollections, and we experience a moral sentiment, which has perhaps some kind of analogy to the physical sensation described by Shakespeare, when he says,

> *The very place puts toys of desperation,*
> *Without more motive, into every brain,*

Connected with this sentiment, those who have witnessed the Revolution feel also a sort of weariness of the memory of what is past. If the succession of time be measured by that of events, we have lived not years, but ages of revolutionary life, and we are tired of the retrospect. In one word, I cannot prevail with myself to go back farther in my narration than the first of March, 1815.

Before I begin, however, let me say a few words of myself; which I shall do with all possible brevity, this being, when we talk of ourselves, the first merit with others. You write to me in something like Italics, as if to give force to reproof, "you *were* a Bonapartist." I shall answer this accusation, by pleading guilty. Yes, I admired Bonaparte; I admired also the French revolution. To my then youthful imagination, the day-star of liberty seemed to rise on the vine-covered hills of France, only to shed benedictions on humanity. I dreamt of prison-doors thrown open,— of dungeons visited by the light of day—of the peasant oppressed no longer—of equal rights, equal laws, a golden age, in which all that lived were to be happy. But how soon did these beautiful illusions vanish, and this star of liberty set in blood! How just was the reflexion of Monsieur Gorani at the time of revolutionary horrors, "*Je connaissais les grands, mais je ne connaissais pas les petits.*" You, however, are not of the number of those who deny that liberty was formed to bless, and dignify mankind, because she has fallen on "*evil days, and evil tongues.*"

When Bonaparte first appeared on the political horizon, I was not yet cured of enthusiasm. He presented himself to the world, as fighting the battles of liberty—and by what splendid victories did he maintain her cause in Italy! What modesty in his demeanour, when, at his return, he made his solemn entry into Paris, and was received at a public audience by the Directory! As he passed through the crowded streets, he leaned back in his carriage, and seemed to shrink from those acclamations which were then the voluntary offering of the heart, and were such as he has since been unable, with all his power, to purchase. I saw him decline placing himself in the chair of state which had been prepared for him, and seem as if he wished to escape from the general bursts of applause.

Allow me to observe also, *en passant*, that I had been assured he was an enthusiastic admirer of Ossian; and when I found that he united to a noble simplicity of character, and a generous disdain of applause, a veneration for Ossian, this circumstance filled up the measure of my admiration. I did not then know that Bonaparte valued Ossian only for his descriptions of battles, like the surgeon who praised Homer only for his skill in anatomy.

Even the events of the 18th *Brumaire*, although somewhat mysterious, were insufficient to shake my credulity. He had dissolved with violence the national representation, but it was only to repress the Jacobins, and prevent the return of terrorism. When he was named First Consul, I believed that liberty was about to flourish fair under his auspices, and that France was henceforth to be great and happy. It seemed as if, in a better sense, it might be said of him, that "*the world was made for Caesar.*" All the circumstances of the Revolution had combined to effect his elevation. The nation was wearied of the great experiment it had made in politics, and for which it had paid so dear. The cruel abuses of liberty, the horrible outrages of the reign of terror were still present to every memory, and even the republicans themselves despaired of a republic. The nation, conscious, at the same time, of the wrongs it had inflicted on the race of its kings, in despair of impunity, added to its offences a new injustice, and believing that the Bourbons would never forget the past, wished to separate them for ever from the future.

In this situation of things, and in this disposition of the public mind, Bonaparte took possession of the government. He had so noble, and so marvellous a part to act, that it was difficult to believe he would mar all by his performance. It might have been expected that he would have had the good taste, as well as morality, to avoid the beaten track of vulgar and ordinary ambition; and that he would seek, by other paths, the prize of purer glory. He soon, however, corrected the defect of discernment in those who had thus augured of his genius, and his virtue. The rapid successive gradations to the consulate for life, and thence to the imperial purple, dispelled all illusion, and displayed the undisguised truth.

Thou hast it now, King, Cawdor, Glamis, all.

Thus ends my confession: and, passing over the memorable interval of time since the coronation of Napoleon the Great, by Pope Pius the Seventh, in the metropolitan church of Notre Dame, let me lead you towards the little vessel on which Bonaparte lately anchored in the bay of Juan.

LETTER 2

April, 1815.
A feeling of surprise, but a very slight degree of inquietude, was

10

excited at Paris, by the intelligence that Bonaparte had landed, on the first of March, at the little town of Cannes, on the coast of Provence, attended by a few followers. His arrival was talked of, less as a subject of alarm, than of speculation with respect to the motives of his expedition. It was generally believed that his appearance in France would be very transient, and that he only meant to open to himself a passage through Piedmont into Italy, to join his brother-in-law Joachim King of Naples.

It seemed indeed singular that he should have landed in Provence, in order to form a junction with Murat at Rome; but as no clearer motive suggested itself to the public mind, this intention was generally admitted. In the meantime, Bonaparte hastened to enlighten the inhabitants of the south with respect to the motive of his visit, declaring that the same sentiments of tenderness and humanity which had induced him to lay aside his imperial authority, at the time when the allies were in possession of Paris and masters of France,—and to which abdication he was compelled by the hope that peace would be restored to this unhappy and desolated country,—had now operated on him to forego the enjoyment of tranquillity, and forsake the rock in the midst of the waves, on which he had suffered exile, in order to rouse the country to a due sense of its inglorious sufferings, and to avenge its wrongs. He promised to restore to France the boundary of the Rhine, to confirm to the people the chart they had adopted, and to reform all the errors of which the reigning powers had been guilty, in their misinterpretation of the articles that had been already discussed.

The tenderness professed by Bonaparte for the people, and his sympathy for their sufferings under the reign of the Bourbons, raised a smile on the lips of the Parisians; yet there were persons who felt their vain-glory awakened by the promises of again extending their frontier to the Rhine, and obliging the Prussians to fall back from the lately ceded territory. The almost universality of France, however, which had groaned so long under the rod of Napoleon, and had blessed its deliverance from his sway, still considered him as the enemy of public and individual repose, and exulted in the hope that this abundant excess of tenderness was about to expose him to the punishment so long due to his crimes; for of his speedy capture there appeared no reasonable cause of doubt.

Whilst the members of the government encouraged this belief in the public, they were not less aware that it was no ordinary disturber with whom they had to deal. It was deemed expedient to assemble all the authorities, civil as well as military. On the 8th March, the Chambers of Peers and of Deputies, which had been prorogued on the last day of the past year to the first of May, were called together for the instant dispatch of business; and the king issued a royal proclamation, in which Napoleon Bonaparte was declared a traitor and a rebel, for having introduced himself by force of arms into the department of the Var, enjoining all civil and military governors, and even private citizens, to lay hands on him, (*de lui courir sus,*) and drag him before a court-martial, to identify his person, and put the law in force against him.

The same punishment was enjoined against the military, and other persons of whatever rank, who shall have accompanied or followed Bonaparte in his invasion of the French territory, unless they submitted within the term of eight days. In this crime were included by the same proclamation, to be punished as its accomplices and adherents, as tending to change the form of government, and provoke civil war, all administrators civil and military, the chiefs as well as those employed in the said administrations, payers and receivers of the public monies, even such private citizens as should directly or indirectly give aid and assistance to the invader.

While the government at Paris was thus employed, Bonaparte, who had assumed the modest title of Lieutenant-General in the name of his son, had trusted but feebly to the effects of his own proclamation. Finding that the provincials near the coast, little solicitous about the liberty and equality he promised to introduce, and still less so for the boundary of the Rhine, were not eager to volunteer their services in his cause, he collected his small band, of six hundred men, and began his march towards Lyons, on his well known and favourite system, *d'aller en avant.*

Bonaparte's march to Lyons, without cavalry, artillery, and other accessories of martial array, appeared to the Parisians so chimerical, that they judged it as impracticable that he should reach Lyons, as that he should march to Paris. They began to wonder that the news of his being taken and destroyed with his small host, of which they were all well assured by private correspondence, was not officially confirmed. The government, which had received no such confirmation, published the assurances of General Marchand, who commanded Grenoble, which was the southern military depot, of the safety of this great station, and the fidelity of the troops.

The garrison of Grenoble construed the word "fidelity" into a different meaning from that of its commander. Bonaparte presented himself at their gates, they fraternized immediately, and not only delivered up the depot, but the general by whom they were commanded. The seventh regiment of the line, commanded by Colonel La Bedoyère, had marched out, and joined Bonaparte on the road between Vizille and Grenoble. Thus M. de la Bedoyère was the first officer who submitted to the invader, and may boast the pre-eminence in treason. Madame de la Bedoyère, of an ancient and honourable family, was so affected by her husband's treachery, that, taking her children with her, she forsook his house, fled to her relations, and left him to enjoy alone his guilty triumph. The division in families is not one of the least evils of civil discord. Its serpents writhe upon the calm bosom of domestic life, and transform all its joys to bitterness. How many near relations have been within this little month thus rudely torn from each other! There is a point in public dissension and public calamity, when the rankled mind revolts at opposition, and the affections of private life seem light in the great balance of destiny.

> *Pour toi, de qui la main sème ici les forfaits,*
> *Et fait naître la guerre an milieu de la paix;*
> *Ton nom seul parmi nous divise les familles,*
> *Les époux, les parens, les mères, et les filles;*
> *La discorde civile est par-tout sur ta trace,*
> *Assemblage inoui de mensonge et d'audace;*
> *Tyran de ton pays, est-ce ainsi qu'en ce lieu*
> *Tu viens donner la paix! &c.*
>
> —*Voltaire*, Mahomet.

The Elbean band, which had hitherto since its landing been wandering among the mountains of the Var, and the departments of the Lower Alps, was now swelled into the appearance of an army, by the junction of the troops at Grenoble. General Marchand, invited by Bonaparte to retake his command, answered, that during his reign as emperor, he had served him with fidelity; that, released from this duty by his abdication, he had sworn allegiance to the existing government; and, presenting his sword, surrendered himself as a prisoner, declaring that he would never be a traitor.

Bonaparte said:

General, I acknowledge your services; I have always looked on you as a true soldier; I see your position, and do not wish you to act contrary to your conscience. Take back your sword, go to Paris, and tell your king, that I shall soon visit him in the capital, arid will treat him with all the consideration due to his virtues and his rank.

The defection of the garrison of Grenoble roused into exertion the government, which had seemed to repose on the terror of its proclamations. *Monsieur*, the king's brother, and the Duke of Orleans, accompanied by Marshal Macdonald, repaired to Lyons, in order to put that city in a state of resistance. Lyons was garrisoned by about two thousand regular troops, and its great population seemed to offer every means of retarding, at least, the progress of the invader; but the only weapons found to arm the inhabitants were three thousand muskets, and these were for the most part unfit for service. The aspect of the city was equivocal with respect to its loyalty, and the regular troops were decidedly in favour of the invader. His appearance before Lyons awakened the cries of *"Vive l'Empereur!"* from the soldiers, in which they were joined by the populace, and he entered without resistance that capital of the Gauls. The French princes retreated to Clermont in Auvergne, and soon after returned to Paris.

Bonaparte had now traversed the country from the coasts to almost the centre of France, without resistance and without firing a shot; and, having enthroned himself at Lyons, threw off the humble air of Lieutenant-General of his son, as well as that of tenderness and sympathy for the sufferings of the nation; and, unable to withstand the salutations of *"Vive l'Empereur!"* by the army, began to issue his imperial decrees with the protocol of:

Napoleon, by the grace of God and the constitutions of the empire, Emperor of the French, &c.

Several changes having been made during his absence in the persons composing his imperial administration both civil and military, he began by decreeing that in the judiciary bodies of every rank, such arbitrary changes were to be regarded as null and void; that all generals and officers who had taken service in the army or navy, and who had been emigrants, should give in their dismission, and return to their homes; that the white cockade and the Order of St. Louis, of the Holy Ghost, and of St. Michael, should be abolished, and that the national three-coloured flag and cockade should only be displayed; that the military establishment of the king should be suppressed; that the goods and chattels of the princes of the house of Bourbon should be sequestrated; that the nobility and feudal titles were abolished; that the emigrants who had entered with the king should quit the French territory; and that the chamber of peers and deputies were dissolved. These imperial dispositions appeared to Bonaparte no doubt necessary to reunite the partisans of his old government; but he could not dissemble to himself that, however agreeable his return might be to the citizens who had revelled in the sweets and emoluments of subordinate power, he had not been happy in securing the assent and affections of any other classes of his subjects. Of this he had been duly informed during his residence in his island of Elba. Every vessel from France that touched his coast had gone laden with pamphlets, all filled with details of his crimes, arraigning him before the present and future ages, and written as if to console and avenge the nation, of which nothing is more remarkable than its physical courage and its moral cowardice, for the silence with which it had borne his oppression. Nothing had been left unsaid; many a terrible truth had been thundered in his ear; many a foot had trampled upon the sick lion; and the revolutionary maxim seemed entirely forgotten, "*qu'il n'y a que les morts qui ne reviennent pas.*" The times were then past when the philosophers and the *litterati* prophaned history, and the clergy Holy Writ, by their strange and grotesque applications.

Bonaparte, conscious that his enchanter's rod was now broken, that he was no longer believed to be invincible, and that he was well known to be guilty, had recourse to new arts. He deemed it necessary to propose a voluntary descent from the height of his ancient dictatorship, and to declare himself the patron and popular chieftain of a free government. He concluded his decree of the suppression of the legislature, by ordering that the:

> Electoral colleges of the departments of the empire should assemble at Paris in the course of next May, *in an extraordinary assembly of the Field of May*, in order to take the measures necessary to correct and modify our constitutions according to the interest and will of the nation, and at the same time to be present at the coronation of the empress, our very dear and well-beloved spouse, and of our dear and well-beloved son.

On the news of the possession of Lyons by Bonaparte and his army, now become formidable by its numbers, consternation began to operate on the Parisian world in the inverse ratio of its former incredulity. The same magical power which had led this extraordinary personage from his island to the canter of France, seemed no less potent to protect his further attempts if it was his intention to wing his way to Paris. There was, however, no supernatural agency in this business; there was nothing even very astonishing in this revolutionary phantasmagoria.

It was scarcely to be imagined that Bonaparte would have thrown himself with so much rashness and precipitation into the midst of France, with a handful of followers,, and have attempted to traverse a country through which, but a few months before, he had passed to his place of exile, loaded with the execrations of its inhabitants, and, even under the protection of his European conquerors, compelled to seek at times his personal safety by assuming the meanest disguises; it could scarcely be imagined that he would have ventured to trace back his steps through this country as a conqueror, and have seated himself in the capital of the south, had he not depended on other forces than those of his followers, and assured to himself other means of success than the riches his Elbean sovereignty afforded. Suspicions arose at Paris that there existed some strange neglect in certain departments of the administrations of government.

It was observed that not only the southern depot of Grenoble had furnished the invader with every implement of war, and that its garrison had shewn a singular alacrity in declaring themselves traitors, but that Lyons had been left without defence, or the arms necessary for the national guard. It seemed strange also that the fleet at Toulon had remained in the harbour, and that, were it merely to exercise the sailors, no cruise had taken place in the space that reaches from the Isle of Elba to the shores of Provence. It is certain that the conspiracy had been carried on during some months, with more good fortune than address. The discovery of one part of the plot was accidental, or, to borrow the pious ejaculation of the new minister of war, seemed to have been made by the miraculous interposition of Providence.

Marshal Mortier, Duke of Treviso, who commanded the troops stationed in the north, had left Paris to return to his headquarters at Lisle, when he met on the indirect road he had taken, a body of troops, consisting of about ten thousand men, on their march to Paris. The astonished marshal demanded where they were going, and found that they had received orders to march upon Paris, to save the city from pillage, and rescue the king from the hands of the populace. He examined the orders, saw they were forgeries, and ordered his soldiers to march back instantly to their quarters.

The town of La Fère, in Picardy, was a northern military depot, under the command of M. D'Aboville. The General Lefèbre Denouettes had entered this town with troops drawn from the garrison of Cambray, under the command of General Lallemand and his brother, demanding military accommodation for two thousand men. The commander of La Fère observed that there was somewhat singular in this march; and having soon obtained proofs of the traitorous intentions of these generals, he put his garrison, at an early hour, in order of battle, and answered the invitation of joining Bonaparte, by the cry of "*Vive le Roi!*" in which he was joined by his troops. The rebel generals sought their safety in flight, but were soon after taken.

Thus Bonaparte's project was neither rash, nor ill-concerted. While he advanced by rapid inarches to Lyons, for which due preparations had been made by the removal of all obstacles, and while the garrison of Grenoble assisted his arrival, his partisans in the north were to furnish him with arms, lead on the troops under their command, and take possession of Paris. The accidental meeting of a powerful detachment of the northern army by Marshal Mortier, and the firmness of D'Aboville at La Fère, disconcerted this part of the plan, but at the same time convinced the government that the conspiracy was not confined to the south, and to the troops that accompanied Bonaparte.

LETTER 3

April, 1815.

The discovery of a conspiracy before it be consummated, is generally considered as the destruction of the enterprise for which it has been formed; but the present plot extended too far to be endangered by the failure of any single ramification. Bonaparte's triumphant march ceased to be marvellous, when it became known that the army was entirely devoted to him; that he had upon his arrival issued his imperial orders to the French troops in all the various stations in the kingdom; that every where the military obeyed him with alacrity, and that this army, like a snow-ball, augmented as it rolled on. The most considerable part of the D French Army, and particularly the imperial guard, had never joined in the execrations with which their chief had been loaded by the French nation. His name, though proscribed, as well as the imperial eagle, were bound to their minds with indissoluble affection; and as they attributed to themselves a share in his military glory, so they had continued to sympathise in his disgrace.

Such were the honourable feelings of a great number; but the most considerable part, who felt not this sort of elevation, remembered, like the Israelites in the Wilderness, the flesh-pots of Egypt, and looked back with regret on those halcyon days when German *burgomasters* and substantial and well prepared repasts awaited their arrival at a town, or village, after the march or combat of the day; and rapine and riot, at the expense of the invaded countries, filled up the intervals of what they styled the career of glory.

A numerous class of the French Army, under the influence of those immoral habits, felt that Bonaparte's banishment had been the death-blow to their hopes, and their enjoyments. With fond regret those heroes of the eagle looked back on the auspicious days in which, till interrupted by the return of peace and the Bourbons, plunder and carnage had been the business of their lives.

Their occupation now was gone—all pomp and circumstance of glorious war!

The whole of the military were thoroughly imbued with the idea that they alone constituted the nation, that they were the first, if not the only, order in the state, and that the rest of the population were the Ilotes, or, in their modern military phraseology, "*péquins*," [1] These Spartans now found themselves sunk in importance, thrown by as encumbrances, and saw with indignation that their profession was dishonoured by the *péquins*, who, under the name of national guards, had devoted themselves to the protection of their country as armed citizens. This military civic spirit, encouraged by the government, had only served to increase the discontent of the regular troops, so that it required no extraordinary effort in Bonaparte's agents to inspire them with the hopes of the return of Saturnian times.

Bonaparte was well apprised of the situation of the army, and of its obedience to his mandate he was no less assured. The chiefs the most devoted to him were of course the only persons initiated in the secret, and to their discretion was entrusted the care of awakening and fostering in their soldiers the glorious hope of new achievements, new honours, and new spoils. With such auxiliaries it required no great effort of courage in Bonaparte to attempt seizing the reins of empire.

1. "I am sorry," said a minister to Marshal L———, "that, after having long waited for you, we are seated at table before you arrive." "I should have come earlier," replied the marshal, "but I have been detained by some, *péquins*" "*Péquins!*" exclaimed the company, "what are *péquins?*" "Oh, you know," rejoined the marshal, "we call *péquins* all that is not military." "Yes," said, the minister, "*comme nous autres nous appellons militaire, tout ce qui n'est pas civil.*"

18

Every necessary precaution had been taken to secure his safety, from the place of his landing, to Lyons. The national guard, indeed, of a little town into which he had entered on his passage, assured the prefect that they could secure him with the greatest ease. The prefect answered that he had received no orders, and refused the proffered aid.

This military conspiracy had some auxiliaries in other classes of the community. There still existed the remains of a party in France which had during a short time wielded the sceptre as despotically as Bonaparte himself. This was the faction of the Jacobins; once no less powerful with the insignia of the red-cap, than Napoleon with his imperial crown, of whom some one, seeing him pass in pomp through the streets of Paris, observed, "*C'est Robespierre à cheval.*" The Jacobins had long been reduced to such death-like silence, that the race was deemed extinct. Bonaparte had received the first rudiment of his political knowledge in their school, and been denominated, by high authority, their child and champion. On his first entrance into power, he adopted the system of fusion, and employed such of the chiefs of the faction as had escaped the scaffold. He was, however, too prudent not to keep the party in proper subjection while he continued to practise their favourite maxim, the secret of all their power, "that of *daring.*"[2] The exile of some of the most turbulent leaders among the populace of the Fauxbourgs, by Bonaparte's orders, had reduced the rest to silence; and though they murmured at his injustice, they dreaded and worshipped his power.

This class was at present too obscure to excite any apprehension in the government; with the exception of a few chiefs, they were to be found only in the poorest of the labouring tribe. They had, however, been useful on some occasions, and in revolutions no means of power ought to be neglected. Subsidies were necessary to raise these dormant allies into action; and subsidies were found by the relations and friends of Bonaparte, and largely distributed by their emissaries.

The tranquil possession of Lyons by Bonaparte, and the increase of his army by deserters from the royal cause, now excited the most serious apprehensions in Paris. The government gave assurances that measures were taken, if Bonaparte should attempt the road of Paris, to cut him off; and preparations were made to collect a formidable army at Melun, a town on the Seine, at the distance of ten leagues from Paris; and another at Montargis, a few hours' march from Fontainbleau.

---

2. *Osez* was declared by one of the Jacobin *coryphées*, in a report to the Convention, to be the secret of all revolutions.

It was asserted that he would soon be placed within two fires, since Marshal Ney had already reached Lons le Saulnier, where an army was stationed, amounting to twelve or fifteen thousand men, with which he was about to fall on his rear.

This officer, who was called the Prince of Moskwa, from the active share he had taken in the combat near that river, had, in an effusion of loyalty, repaired to the Tuileries, and proffering his services, had assured the king, on receiving the command of this important station, that he would bring Bonaparte to Paris in an iron cage. To which the king replied, with mild dignity, that this was not what he required, and that he only desired of the marshal to drive back the invader. The Prince de la Moskwa took his leave of the king, carried with him a million of *livres* for the pay of the troops, and departed.

Though it was greatly apprehended that the spirit of disaffection had pervaded the army in general, it was hoped that a part would yet be found *"faithful among the faithless."* The knowledge that armies were placed in front, on the flanks, and in the rear, cheered the drooping spirits of the Parisians, who, applauding the loyalty of the national guard, rather than confiding in their prowess, saw with satisfaction the departure of the marshals to head the armies, and particularly of the Prince de la Moskwa, whose assurances to the king were cited in his own phraseology, that he would bring the Sovereign of Elba, in an iron cage, to Paris.

Bonaparte meanwhile, after haranguing the people of his good city of Lyons, took an affectionate leave of the citizens, and proceeded on his way to Paris. Traversing Macon, Tournus, and Autun, he reached Auxerre, where he was immediately joined by Marshal Ney, with his whole division, and whom he had ordered to hoist the three-coloured flag. A part of this division was well disposed toward the king, and the troops would probably have done their duty, had they not been surprised into treason. Marshal Ney issued at Lons le Saulnier the following proclamation:

> Officers and Soldiers! the cause of the Bourbons is for ever lost. The lawful dynasty, which the French nation has adopted, is about to ascend the throne. It is to the Emperor Napoleon alone, our sovereign, that belongs the right of reigning over our fine country, &c. Soldiers, I have often led you to victory, I will now lead you to join that immortal *phalanx* which the Emperor Napoleon is conducting to Paris, and which will be there in a

few days, and there our hopes, and our happiness, will be for ever realised.

Vive l'Empereur!

(Signed)   The Prince of Moskwa.

Such have been the vicissitudes of opinion, and the changes of the political creed of individuals, amidst the various phases of the French Revolution, that considerable allowances may be made for many; but no morality however lax, no charity however lenient, can forbear stigmatizing, with eternal ignominy, the conduct of certain actors in this turbulent drama:—at the head of this black column must be inscribed the name of the Prince of Moskwa. The services of this marshal were not demanded; they were offered with an exuberance of zeal for the royal cause, and his ardour was repressed rather than excited by the king, to whom he gave with eagerness the sacred pledge of his honour.

When the tidings of this fatal disaffection reached Paris, when it was known that this great division of the army, on which all the public hope reposed, had gone over to the invader, horror and despair filled every bosom. Unavailing execrations against such black perfidy, as that of Marshal Ney, hung upon every lip; and the red iron, with which he is condemned to be marked in history, seemed a slight compensation for the wrongs of his injured country.

Napoleon entered Fontainbleau on the 20th March, at four in the morning. He learnt that the Bourbons had quitted Paris, and that the capital was free. With his accustomed superstition for particular days, he remembered also, that this was the birthday of the King of Rome; he therefore departed immediately, determined to enter Paris that evening.

Thus, in the space of three short weeks, did this daring soldier transfer the seat of empire from his rocky exile to the palace of the Tuileries. We saw him seated on his throne, and we believed it to be almost a delusion of our senses. The rapidity of his march appears a prodigy of which history offers no example; the enterprise seems unparalleled in all that is great and daring; and his pacific triumph bears the stamp of the general assent of the nation. Such conclusions would, however, be most erroneous. There was nothing miraculous in his journey. He was quietly conveyed to Paris in his *calèche*, drawn by four post-horses, which he found prepared at every relay; and it required but ordinary courage to advance through a country where all that was hostile to his purpose were defenceless and unarmed, and all that could have opposed his progress hailed him with acclamations of transport.

But if the triumphal march of Napoleon Bonaparte, from the coast of Provence to the capital of France, presents, when investigated in its details, no marvel to the imagination, it teaches, at least, a most tremendous lesson to mankind; it adds a new page of instruction on the danger of military influence; it shews us that no other ties are so powerful as those which bind the soldier to his chief. What the French Army would have called rebellion was resistance to the voice of their general. The military ravagers of other countries can never become the civic defenders of their own. Their bosoms beat high with the inextinguishable hope of what mankind, in its hour of madness, has agreed to call by the name of glory.

They had acquired under Bonaparte that fatal ascendant which led them to consider even their own country as their conquest. Careless of its miseries, forming a class apart from their fellow-citizens, like the *Janizaries* of the east, or the *Praetorian* bands of the Roman empire, they consulted only their own triumph, and disposed of crowns and sceptres at their will. The land which gave them birth, and which they were destined to defend, they have covered with desolation, and have opened an abyss to France from which the heart recoils, and where the eye fears to penetrate.

LETTER 4

May, 1815.

Gloomily arose the morning of the 20th March on the inhabitants of Paris. It was known that Louis XVIII. had left his capital at midnight, and no heart was unmoved by the affecting detail of his departure. The national guard at the Tuileries melted into tears at the sight of their unfortunate monarch as he descended the steps of the *château*, knelt as he passed through their ranks, pressed to their lips his hands, even the flaps of his coat, and, conjuring him not to depart, declared that they were ready to sacrifice their lives in his defence. The king endeavoured to calm their emotion by expressing his belief that he should again return to the palace of his fathers, while the Comte d'Artois, deeply dejected, mingled his tears with those of these faithful citizens.

During the preceding day, the people of Paris had been agitated by doubt, fear, hope, and expectation. But the fatal certainty had not reached them. Their king was a fugitive, and the tyrant was hastening to fill the vacant throne. He drew nearer every minute; resistance was forbidden because it was useless, and Paris was once more destined to bend her prostrate head to the dust. Peace, commerce, security, fortune, children, all that binds the human heart to existence, all that cheers and gives it value was again to be sacrificed at the shrine of the usurper. Early in the morning the shopkeepers were busily employed in changing their signs. Every where the crested lily disappeared, and the victorious eagle again stretched over the portals his terrific wings.

The northern *boulevard*, from the gates of St. Denis and St. Martin to the Barrier, was crowded in the afternoon by Bonaparte's allies, the mob of the eastern Fauxbourgs. Many hideous figures had crept from their holes, on this triumphant occasion; and as a refreshing subsidy had been distributed to these new sovereigns, they had qualified themselves by intoxication to share in the benefit of the "*joyeuse entrée.*" Paris had not been affrighted by such appearances, male and female, since the days of their former reign in the time of terror, when their ministry had been actively employed and duly rewarded as revolutionary committee-men, attendants at the daily assassinations, and what was called "*les tricoteuses de la guillotine*," on account of their practice of knitting at the foot of the scaffold while they were waiting for the sad spectacle.

It required all the vigilance of the national guard of the city to keep the semblance of order; for the few regular troops who remained in Paris, ashamed of such confederates, disdained the occupation. The day closed, and Napoleon had not yet appeared. He was aware of the greetings that awaited him, and lingered on the road till night should screen his entry and save him the disgrace of such a reception. The mob, or such at least as could yet vociferate "*Vive l'Empereur*," remained at their posts; while he, traversing other streets than those in which he was expected, arrived at nine in the evening at the palace of the Tuileries.

No one in this inconstant nation changes with more dexterity than a journalist. He is always prepared for a *coup de théâtre*, a sudden change of scene. Whatever power prevails, he instantly respects its authority, and seizes eagerly the permission to become its slave. The 21st March, the newspapers, bearing the stamp of the eagle, proclaimed in pompous style the entry of the Emperor Napoleon on the preceding evening in his capital.

23

Tumult and disorder prevailed in the streets, which were soon filled with newly arrived troops, and the soldiers and populace were alike decorated with a bunch of violets.

That lovely and earliest flower of spring, the symbol of timid beauty, and the soft harbinger of summer, had been transformed into the badge of a sanguinary faction. The military, who were initiated in the secret of Bonaparte's intended return in spring, had applied to him the nickname of *Le Père la Violette*. Rings of a violet colour had been worn by his party, and the name of the violet was pronounced with other words of mysterious import, and veiled, like the modest flower itself, from general observation. But on the morning of the 21st March, the guilty, the triumphant violet appeared glaring in the button-hole of every Bonapartist's coat, or stuck into his hat, with all the ostentation of an order, or a cockade. After such a profanation, how many springs must pass over the violet before its character will be retrieved, and its purity appear unsullied!

It had been the policy of the Bourbons to depress, as far as possible, that dangerous spirit which pervaded the soldiery in favour of their old leader. This, which was a wise and necessary policy, not only for their own personal repose, but that of the country, served unhappily to increase the hostile dispositions of the military. They beheld not only the whole of their importance vanished as the first body of the state, but saw that all personal confidence on the part of the king was withheld from them. Louis the XVIIIth had formed his military establishment of *gardes du corps, mousquetaires*, and Swiss regiments, composed of men who had not served in the armies of the late emperor.

This measure was blamed by those who asserted that had the king confided his person to the care of the imperial guard, flattered by such a mark of confidence, and called upon by honour to justify it, they would never have betrayed their trust. This might be true of the greater number, but perhaps not of all; and the chance was scarcely to be risked in a circumstance so important, and where an error of opinion would have been fatal.

This avowed dissatisfaction of the military was highly favourable to the plans of Bonaparte, and was promoted by his emissaries in almost every corps, who were taught to raise their views to brighter destinies, and who were flattered with the hope that a day of new glories might soon again break on them with renovated splendour. No correspondence had been for a long time more active than that of Paris and Porto Ferrajo, and its frequency seemed to pass unnoticed by the government.

At the review which took place the day after his arrival, Napoleon, addressing the soldiers, told them that he had landed with only six hundred men, because he had relied on the affection of his people, and on the remembrance of his old soldiery; that he had not been disappointed; that he thanked them; and that this new-acquired glory belonged to them and to the people.

Soldiers, added Bonaparte, the throne of the Bourbons is illegitimate, since it has been erected by foreign hands, proscribed by the voice of the nation expressed in every national assembly, and offering no guarantee except to a small number of arrogant men whose pretensions are hostile to its rights. Soldiers, the imperial throne alone can guarantee the rights of the people, and especially the first of interests, that of our glory. We are going to march to drive from our territory those princes, the auxiliaries of foreigners; the nation will not only aid us with its vows, but will follow the impulse we shall give it. The French people and myself rely on you. We will not interfere in the affairs of other nations, but woe to those that interfere with our own.

Such was Bonaparte's first confession of faith at the Tuileries, and which was well suited to such an auditory as his soldiers, who desired to hear of nothing more agreeable than the project to march *en avant*, and who highly relished the idea of the blessings of a foreign campaign.

But although in possession of the seat of empire, Bonaparte did not dissemble to himself that he had already a formidable foe to combat, which was public opinion; and though he could not confirm the first falsehood he had published, that of the twenty years' truce, which he had brought in his pocket, he did not hesitate to affirm that he fully expected, on his return, the general acquiescence of Europe. His partisans proclaimed that Austria, in sending back the empress and the young Napoleon, evidently proved that it was friendly to the cause of the invasion. It was equally clear that the English commissary at the Isle of Elba had connived, by his opportune absence, at the escape of Bonaparte; and that the progress of French manufactures, and other causes of national jealousy, would lead England to foment disturbances in France, and would render it very lukewarm in the support of a new coalition; that the forces of the Russian Empire were beyond the Vistula, the finances of that power could not permit any great efforts, and it was also too much occupied with its internal affairs and new acquisitions, to be at all interested in French concerns.

The German princes would follow the example of Austria; so

that the only power that could be earnest in the contention would be Prussia, with whom it would be easy to arbitrate. It cannot be supposed that Bonaparte's ministers, or his council of state, were the dupes of these reasonings, or that they gave credit to any of his assertions respecting the friendly dispositions of the princes of Europe. They had been long habituated to his impostures, and were at no pains to conceal their opinion of the flimsiness of the foundations on which he built his hopes, the fallacy of his arguments, and the inevitable evils which his precipitancy had brought on himself and the country. One of his ministers, he whose opinions had the greatest weight, both with Bonaparte and with the French of all parties, who knew with the most dexterity how "*to strip the gilding off the knave*," far from concealing the truth, in these discussions, always finished by the assertion, "*enfin, vous êtes un homme perdu.*"

While this debate on probabilities was yet carrying on in the divan of the Tuileries, a decree of the Congress of the 10th March arrived, and put to flight the fairy visions of peace, by the intelligence that the empress and her son were detained at Schoenbrunn. Such was the result of the twenty years' truce, of the announced coronation of his wife, and son, and of the Austrian alliance!

Bonaparte could not parry this stroke. He now stood before his ministers and council convicted of deceit and falsehood. He had committed not only the safety of the army and of France, but what was of some import with these ministers and counsellors, their own personal safety, and their fortunes. His blusterings and his rhapsodies were no longer the bursts of thunder; he shrunk at the menacing look and retort of the ministers, and was obliged to solicit advice, and pray for counsel, which it was no longer dangerous to give to the chief who had forty legions at his orders.

In the meantime, the people of Paris were filled with consternation at the evils with which they were menaced. The twenty years' truce in Bonaparte's pocket had never been believed an instant, except by a few of the lowest class; the royalists wept over the fall of the monarchy, and the republicans felt no great confidence in assurances of liberty and rights that were to be guaranteed only by imperial authority.

In this hour of calamity, one only hope of deliverance visited the bosoms of the Parisians; it was a melancholy hope, and wore something of the sickly hue of despair; this was no other than the determined resistance of the allied powers of Europe to the usurper. Alas! to what wretchedness is that unhappy country reduced, which is compelled to wish for the intervention of foreigners to avenge its wrongs! The allied powers declared that they would approach as the friends of France, and that they only made war against its tyrant. But it could not be dissembled that a million of friends in arms, with a cortege of bayonets, cannon, bombs, shells, and Congreve rockets, came at least in questionable shape, and that the visit had a formidable aspect.

The character of the generous monarchs who led on these innumerable hosts, was indeed well calculated to inspire security. Their conduct last year had been so highly philanthropic, that they had themselves formed a new precedent of generosity, which already belonged to history, and which must be henceforth the rule of future conquerors, who would avoid the eternal reproaches of mankind; but if in the ordinary state of the world, there may be perhaps a greater portion of distress than of pity, how could it be hoped that general benevolence would exclude partial evil in circumstances so extraordinary? How difficult to say to the tempest of war, *thus far shalt thou go, and no farther!*

In the meantime, society in the *salons* of Paris avenged itself of the government, by the most bitter animadversions on all that passed; and the downfall of the usurper was predicted with certainty in all good company. If Bonaparte could still boast of partisans among the men, it is at least certain that he found few among the women.

That sex, which in this country has so powerful an influence on the great as well as the little interests of society, had long since declared against him. With the exception of a few ladies of Napoleon's court, which, on account of its military composition, might have been properly called his camp, and a few of the lowest class, the women of France were unanimously royalists. Every sentiment of female nature might indeed be naturally supposed to be averse to a system of tyranny and blood; but these feelings belonged not, in this instance, to a vague, general opinion. The women of France had found tyranny brought home to their very bosoms;[3] its "*iron had entered into their souls.*" They had felt it poisoning the sweetness of domestic life, shedding bitterness over all its charms, and blasting all its enjoyments. Who had not wept

---

3. The *prefects* had secret orders to send lists of the most wealthy young ladies of their respective departments. Their parents then received what was called an invitation, which meant an order, to consent to their marriage with certain military favourites, who possessed nothing but the Iron Crown, and the order of the Legion of Honour. Many of these marriages took place; and the most opulent merchants and bankers of Paris, in giving their daughters, found their strong chests also put in requisition, and consigned to the discretion of their sons-in-law.

for a brother, an affianced lover, a husband, or a son? Who had not lamented the years of youth wasted without hope, or those of mature age without consolation?

How many Rachaels mourned for their children, and would not be comforted because they were not? Conscription—what a terrible word!—How little you can feel, or comprehend all its meaning!—Oh no! it has drawn no tears from your eyes it has awakened no anguish in your bosom! They only understand it well, whose children have been exposed to its savage grasp. You know that I have adopted since their infancy my two nephews, the children of my only sister; you have not forgotten Cecilia, who in dying left them to my care.

I have educated, and loved them, not with what is called instinctive fondness, which perhaps is an illusion, but with the steadfast affection of long habit, which binds us by such endearing ties to the objects we have reared and cherished. If there is something more tender in nature than the sentiment I feel for them, they know it not, for they can recollect no mother but myself, and therefore they reward my cares with all the feelings of filial attachment. My nephews then are unto me as children! They are the dear relics of her who was born my friend, and whose loss was the more irreparable, since the friends acquired in a foreign country, however valuable, are not those of infancy, not those to whom it can be fondly said, "we grew together." My eldest nephew had attained the fatal age in the beginning of March, 1814, and was forced to draw his lot as a conscript. He was exempted as being a student in theology, in the new protestant college of Montauban, but this was only a reprieve; and this year, had not Bonaparte been overthrown, he, as we'll as all the other students, would probably have been compelled to leave their college, and take up arms. Had the same tyranny continued to prevail, the same fate would have awaited his brother.

A thousand little mystic inventions, contrivances of the heart, were employed by the women, expressive of their opinions, and affections; and in which *"more was meant than met the ear."* Many a sign was given, and received, which, like that of the Free-masons, was only known to the initiated. The colour of a flower, or a ribbon, became an affair of state; the perfumes of the violet were held in as much abhorrence as if they had shed the poisons of the Upas; and not only the devoted lily, but all white flowers being forbidden, the colour generally adopted by the Parisian ladies, was blue, the royal colour, and the symbol of constancy. New royalist songs were every day written, and adapted to simple well-known airs, in which all could join. These songs flew like electric fire through Paris; how many rosy lips repeated, with fond enthusiasm, the favourite close, "*il reviendra!*" Chamfort long since observed of France, that it was "*une monarchie absolue, tempérée par des chansons.*" But it was not in the polite circles only of the Fauxbourg St. Germain, (the west-end of the town of Paris,) that the women flocked round the white standard of the Bourbons. Les Dames de la Halle, the Covent-Garden of that city, were also the declared adherents of the race of their kings. Daring indeed would have been that man, and fearless of female vengeance, who would have ventured to apostrophise one of those ladies by the opprobrious appellation of "*une dame de la violette,*" the epithet given to the Bonapartists. The women of the Halle recollected or at least knew by tradition of many ancient privileges which had belonged to their order; such as presenting themselves on certain days at court, and of offering bouquets to their sovereign on joyous or solemn occasions. They remembered too the halcyon times when sugar and coffee were cheap, and their cups overflowed with that reviving beverage.

The women of this class also were wives, and mothers—they too had suffered the pang of separation; they had bid the last farewell to their sons; they also knew, to use the words of the orator, "*what a parent feels, when deprived of the hope of dying before her child.*"—Les Dames de la Halle, who discussed together the great events that were passing, in tones too loud and language too offensive to be tolerated by the government, received an intimation that those who talked politics would lose their places, which here depend upon the police, the regulator of all human affairs in this country; watching over all, the great and the minute, and surveying alike what passes under the painted roofs of the palace, and the umbrella-sheds of the market-place. The ladies of the Halle, however, found a means of declaring their sentiments, by singing continually a favourite air, in which the burden of the song consisted of a play upon words, and might be read, "*Donnez-nous notre pair de gants*"—or, "*Donnez-nous notre Père de Gand!*"—(Ghent.) The police heard in silence this *jeu de mots*, which was beyond the pale of its jurisdiction, and subject to no pains or penalties.

LETTER 5

May, 1815.

M. de Buffon observes, that the most ferocious wolf when taken in a snare becomes the most affrighted and cowardly of animals, and suffers himself to be chained without resistance. Such was now the situation of Bonaparte. His ministers were the masters of his fate, and would perhaps at this moment have saved their country, had they not feared his allies of the Fauxbourgs and the army.

He was, however, made to understand that he must lay aside past illusions; that the shouts of the soldiery or the mob were no proofs of popularity; that he must be conscious of being regarded with horror by the generality of the French nation; and that he could only maintain his power by renouncing the opinions on which he had founded and exercised his authority; and by a speedy return to the original principles of the French revolution.

The class of politicians who supported these principles was Bonaparte's insurmountable aversion: they had indeed submitted, like others, to his imperial mandates, but they still fostered rebellious opinions, and were out of the pale of that principle of unity, which was the name he gave to his own despotism. He attributed to these *ideologues* every mishap. Ideology had been the cause of the failure of the attack on Russia, as he formally declared to the senate on his return from that expedition. His war against ideology was incessant, and his hatred inveterate; but now, seeing that his own counsellors were become the proselytes of this doctrine, he appeared to capitulate, upon the condition, that, as the people were to be sovereigns, he should at least retain the title of sovereign over them.

This new profession of political faith was promulgated to the public a few days after Bonaparte's arrival at the Tuileries, in the form of an extract from the register of the deliberations, declaring that:

> The Council of State, on resuming its functions, deems it to be its duty to make known the principles which are the rules of its opinions, and its conduct.

This preamble was judged necessary to instruct the public that the council of state were free to have principles, and to act accordingly. It was also a kind of responsibility, or caution for Bonaparte's better conduct. Then follows the ideology—

> The sovereignty resides in the people; the people is the only lawful source of power.
> In 1789, the people regained its rights, which had been for so long a time usurped, or unacknowledged.

The extract from the deliberations continued to state, that:

> The feudal monarchy had been abolished by the National As-

30

sembly, and that a constitutional monarchy and a representative government had taken its place; that the resistance of the Bourbons to these national decrees had occasioned their fall, and banishment; and that the people, by its votes, had twice consecrated the new form of government established by its representatives.

Here ended the history of popular government, and of the constitutional labours of the National Assemblies. Bonaparte is then brought on the scene. The council continues to state, that in the eighth year of the republic, Bonaparte, already crowned by victory, was raised to the government by the assent of the nation, and that a constitution created the consular magistracy; that in the tenth year, he was appointed, by a senatorial decree, consul for life; and that in the twelfth year, another senatorial decree conferred on Napoleon the imperial dignity, and made it hereditary in his family. These solemn acts were submitted to the acceptation of the people, and consecrated by near four millions of votes.

Thus ended the council of state's history of Bonaparte's usurpation; which was glossed over as decently as the circumstances admitted: it was not the moment to confess to the nation, that this *epocha* had marked its utter degradation; that it had been then despoiled of its sovereignty; that its consecration of the imperial dignity by its vote was a mockery; and that the imperial years following the usurpations of the fourth and twelfth years, had been marked by every turpitude, crime, tyranny and disgrace that could afflict a country.

These truths were not indeed withheld in the discussions at the Tuileries, although the respective situation of the parties rendered the promulgation imprudent. The council of state concluded this historical sketch by animadversions on the Bourbons.

The Bourbons had ceased to reign in France for twenty-two years; they were forgotten by their contemporaries, and were strangers to our laws, institutions, manners and glory: unknown to the present generation, they were remembered only by the wars they had excited against the country, and the internal discords they had occasioned.

France was invaded in 1814, and the capital taken. Foreigners created a provisional government, assembled the minority of the senate, and forced it, against its mission, and its will, to destroy the existing constitutions, to overturn the imperial throne, and recall the family of the Bourbons; the senate, having been instituted only for the preservation of the constitutions of the empire, had no power to change them, but it decreed that Louis Stanislas Xavier should be proclaimed King of the French, as soon as he should have accepted the constitution, sworn to respect it, and cause it to be respected.

There was a part of the history, which, however disagreeable to record, it was yet essential to mention;—this was the state of affairs when the allies took possession or the capital, and when Bonaparte had been compelled to throw off the imperial robe.

These counsellors say:

The abdication of the Emperor Napoleon was the result only of the unhappy situation to which France and the emperor had been reduced by the events of the war, by treasons, and the occupation of the capital. The sole object of the abdication was to avoid civil war, and the effusion of blood. This act, not sanctioned by the votes of the people, could not destroy the solemn contract formed between them and the emperor; and also, though Napoleon might have been able to abdicate the crown personally, he could not sacrifice the rights of his son, called to reign after him.

This knotty point of the abdication was presumed by these casuists to have been tolerably resolved, and the incident of defeat was as gently glided over as the remembrance of so unfortunate an event could have admitted. The humane motives for the former, namely, Napoleon's repugnance of shedding French blood, the solemn contract between the emperor and the people, and his abdication not having received the sanction of their votes, were deemed at first too hazardous to publish. It was, however, at length decided to be as safe to mock the people, as to enslave them, and the rhodomontade of tenderness, solemn contracts, and unsanctioned abdication, was suffered to remain. How naturally do these serpentine politics remind one of the reflexion of the celebrated M. ———! "*J'ai un dégoût de l'histoire, quand je pense que, ce que nous faisons aujourd'hui, sera un jour de l'histoire.*"

These counsellors continued:

The emperor, in again ascending the throne to which the people had raised him, re-established their most sacred rights. He is called to sanction anew by institutions, (and he has taken the engagement in his proclamations to the nation, and the army, to do so,) all liberal principles, personal liberty, and equality of rights; the freedom of the press, liberty of worship, the vote of taxes by the commons, national property, the independence of courts of justice, and the responsibility of ministers, and of every agent of the executive power.

Such are the principles by which the council of state decides that the nation shall be governed, and such the conditions laid on him whom the people are said to have called to govern them. But we order, for the more effectual preservation of the rights and obligations of the people, that the national institutions be renewed in a great assembly, already convoked by the emperor.

The council concluded this important deliberation, by intimating, that:

Until the meeting of this great representative assembly, the emperor ought to exercise, conformably to the constitution and laws existing, the powers which have been delegated to him, which cannot be taken from him, which he could not abdicate without the consent of the nation, and which the desire and general interest of the French people make it his duty to resume.

To give this declaration the greater force, it was signed individually by the council of state, who seemed to have become the guarantees of Bonaparte's good conduct till the assembly of the Field of May, which was to consist of the electors from every department of the empire, the immediate representatives of the people in primary assemblies, and whose votes were to be regarded as their voice.

Whatever share of credulity may belong to the French character, scarcely any party yielded faith to the professions of the council or the conversion of their chief. Every gift from his hands was regarded with distrust. The great mass of the citizens of France admitted not the possibility of Bonaparte's reformation, and saw nothing but slavery in the revival of Jacobinism, and its junction with imperialism.

The speculative partisans of these different opinions formed but an inconsiderable number in the mass. The proceedings of the council of state, which were intended to renew the primitive spirit of the Revolution, failed entirely. Their reversion to past principles was scoffed at by all parties, and little heed was given to their charges against the Bourbons. It was not considered, by candid and liberal minds, as a crime in the royal family of France, that with the feelings common to human nature, they indulged a predilection for those persons who had followed their destinies, and shared their misfortunes. Yet it is difficult to believe how small was the number of those true followers, "*faithful found, among the faithless.*" The great mass of emigrants had long preceded their sovereign in his entry into France; they had, for the most part, eagerly accepted the amnesty of Napoleon, and some of the most illustrious names of France had been for years attached to his service.

It was indeed lamented, that the king, with every disposition to diffuse happiness around him, sometimes mistook the means, and viewed the situation of the country, through the medium of his ministers, unused to revolutionary politics. A free press, it was observed, was equally the safeguard of the prerogative of the crown, and the rights of the people. The Chart had proclaimed this liberty of the press, but it was explained, and as it were nibbled away, by ministerial misinterpretation, in the legislative discussion on this subject, and was still more reduced in the execution. No newspaper was published without the imprimatur of a censor, named by ministers; and the king was left ignorant of apprehensions, and abuses, which his own good understanding would have led him to calm, and correct.

The people in general, while sufficiently indifferent to the discussion of abstract opinions, were extremely tenacious of their property; and the reports of the intended spoliation of what was called national property, the re-establishment of tythes, and the restoration of the former ecclesiastical domains, was a calumny, which had been propagated by Bonaparte's partisans with more industry and effect than any other. More than half of the population of France was interested in the disposal of the national property, on account of the various channels through which it had flowed since the first purchasers; but none would have been more deeply affected by such a measure, than the class of the poor, among whom the minor domains of the church had been divided.

In France there is no provision for the poor, except by hospitals in large towns, and what are called Committees of Beneficence, the sparing funds for which arise from the *octrois*, or taxes on provisions, levied at the gates of towns. These funds were distributed by the minister of the interior, on the demands of the *prefects*, were often converted to the uses of the army by Bonaparte. Before the Revolution, the church had distributed these alms, and its ministers had necessarily acquired considerable influence over the numerous class of the poor. On the disposal of church-property by the state, in the first years of the Revolution, that which lay in the vicinity of small towns, and villages, was divided among the poorer inhabitants, so that each family became proprietor of half an acre, or an acre, whereon to feed a cow, or raise vegetables, the produce of which land, cultivated by the family at leisure hours, bestowed independence, raised it above the humiliation of receiving charity, and rendered poor's-rates useless.

The order of the priesthood had lost both its influence and its wealth; and, it must be admitted, had sunk below its due rank in society. The prospect of an amelioration under a government, the chiefs of which were known to possess a deep sentiment of piety, had led these long-humbled ecclesiastics to the retrospect of more brilliant times; and some had imprudently indulged in prognostications which had alarmed their flocks with the fear of being compelled to render their little pastures and gardens.

The priest had become the willing, but innocent agent of this calumny, invented by the enemies of the Bourbons, whose intentions of restoring tythes and church property were widely and sedulously extended. The doctrine of tythes was proclaimed from some village pulpits, though no instance is recorded where such restitutions were exacted; but apprehension had the same effect as the actual spoliation: and in the supposed overweening attachment of the Bourbons to the church, for which, in fact, all they had done since their late accession, was to have given an example of piety, the peasant was taught to foresee the loss of that little cherished spot, which he had cultivated with the sweat of his brow, and which he regarded with honest pride, as the inheritance of his family.

Were the charges brought against the Bourbons minutely examined, they would, for the greater part, be found equally devoid of truth, with that respecting churchlands, and tythes. These calumnies were, nevertheless, productive of serious mischief, as they affected a very numerous class of the people, who had no leisure for examination, and fewer means than any other, of being undeceived.

But whatever were the differences of opinion with respect to the proposed regeneration of the French Government, there was a most cordial concurrence of sentiment respecting the chief himself. Everyone beheld Bonaparte smiling, under his air of penitence, at the toil and trouble of these new constitution-makers, bidding them good speed till they had again confirmed him in the possession of his throne, and then, like another Sampson, whose locks had escaped their sheers,

35

and laughing loud at their credulity, he would probably snap at once all the chains of popular sovereignty, laws, equality, and rights of man, and brandishing his imperial eagle, would rally his troops around him, and perhaps send his council of state to dig his iron mines at Elba.

LETTER 6

May, 1815,

His Imperial Majesty had scarcely passed his probationary week of fraternisation at Paris, with the majesty of the populace, ere he began to shew dissatisfaction at the familiar tone of this new acquaintance, to which, on his conversion, he had been introduced by his ministers. He had hitherto been hailed with flattering vociferation only by his soldiers, who were his immediate dependants; and the only part of the people who had thrown up their caps, were those of the lowest class. When they resorted to the Tuileries at the intervals, or daily close of their labours, they assembled under Napoleon's apartments, and bawled out loudly for his appearance. The emperor obeyed the summons; but, wearied with these demonstrations of fraternity, and viewing through his spying-glass the quality of his greeters, expressed his disgust at the impudence of the *canaille*, since he perceived that none above that rank had deigned to salute him.

The theatres had commonly been the scenes of popular shoutings, in the imperial days of former times, and by the management of the police, the hired plaudits had been tolerably successful. It was however thought too hazardous to resort to this expedient in the present circumstances, lest indecent opposition, or gloomy silence, should mar the exhibition. But scarcely had a fortnight elapsed, ere the enthusiasm of the military, as well as that of the populace, had entirely vanished. The former had learned that, instead of full pay, and either a twenty years' truce, or a summer's promenade through Germany, they should be compelled to march against their rebel countrymen in the south or west, or face myriads pouring down from the north with no prospect of pay, or plunder, and with the chance of being exterminated.

The populace began now to discover that their work-shops were closed, and that these shouts of "Long life to the Emperor" were likely to shorten their own, and that of their families. These allies of imperial power, and glory, began to waver in their politics, and meditate on the prospect of starving for want of employment, or of fighting for interests not their own.

This dissatisfaction was not unobserved by the ministers. It was, however, still necessary to keep up the fever of popularity, and the Field of May was again brought forward. It was publicly announced that the minister of the interior had issued his instructions to the prefects of the departments, to prepare the electoral colleges for this extraordinary assembly. It was urged by the minister that this decree for the convocation was an homage tendered to the great and eternal principles which constitute civilized states; and which, though obscured, or stifled by feudal anarchy, had resumed new force and splendour in modern times; and whose long duration was in future assured by the progress of light and knowledge. The minister adds:

> It was for these principles that France raised itself in 1789; for these that she fought against all Europe; and their acquisition is associated with the unparalleled glory of the French armies. The emperor acknowledges those rights of the people, obtained by a war of twenty-five years, and rejects the maxim, that the nation is made for the throne, and not the throne for the nation.
>
> What a sublime and glorious spectacle, is that of a hero, the idol of a people which had conquered Europe, declaring that from them and his soldiers he holds his power; that he will reign only by the laws; and that, in concurrence with the deputies of the nation, he is going, by vigorous and wise institutions, to lay the foundation of monarchical power, with the independence of a free and enlightened nation!

This prospect of regeneration was hailed with no raptures by the departments; the revolutionary spirit had evaporated; and the greater part thought more of preservation, and of defence against Bonaparte and his abettors, than of discussing first principles, and recommencing the Revolution. The south of France had continued to wear the form of resistance. Marseilles, Valence, and others had marshalled a small force to act under the orders of the Duke of Angouleme; while Bordeaux, Toulouse, and the countries bordering on the Pyrenees, shewed their disaffection, by remaining in a state of defenceless opposition. It may be observed, that since the Revolution, partial insurrections have never succeeded against the capital, but have always yielded to seduction or terror. Some hopes had been entertained that the efforts of the Duchess of Angouleme would have been supported by some aid from the allied powers. A few regiments, it was asserted, headed by an experienced commander, would have rallied the whole of the population which remained uncertain, because they had no point of union. The princess herself was the most active of the southern chiefs; she had marshalled the inhabitants of Bordeaux, and was always the first in the council, or the field.

The Duchess of Angouleme had not been spared by the Bonapartists, amidst the censures heaped upon her family. One of the heaviest charges brought against her was the habitual melancholy of her disposition; she was found guilty of having no French gaiety in her character. The Parisians remembered not that this princess, at an age when the heart is already susceptible of deep, and lasting impressions, had seen her whole family perish, and had herself been led from the gloomy tower of her prison, into an exile which had lasted twenty years; that on returning to the palace of her fathers, it was natural that some melancholy reflections should darken for her the triumphal pomp, and mingle themselves with the exultation of her joy. But sadness was not the sole offence of the Duchess of Angouleme; her extreme piety was declared to be fitter for a monastery than a court; and in the caricatures of the royal family which filled the print-shops after their departure, she was always placed on her knees before a *prie-dieu*, as if incapable of all other occupations.

But no less was the confusion of her adversaries, than the triumph of her adherents, when it was announced in Paris, that this princess, with that energy which, in a superior mind, is called forth by extraordinary situations, had risen from her knees, and invoking in her heart the aid of heaven, had mounted on horseback, rid every day through the ranks, and displayed a courage worthy of heroic times. When Bonaparte sent a considerable detachment to march against her, she ordered a general to conduct her to the Château de la Trompette. The general hesitated, assuring her that she would be in danger. "I do not ask you sir," said she, "if there would be danger, I only order you to conduct me." She rode up to a circle of officers on the esplanade, whom she harangued, exhorting them to fidelity and the renewal of their oaths of allegiance in presence of the enemy.

Observing their coldness, and hesitation, she exclaimed, "I see your fears, you are cowards; I absolve you from your oaths already taken!" and turning her horse, she left them, and immediately embarked on board an English frigate. The inhabitants of Bordeaux followed her to the seashore, with fond enthusiasm, with lamentations, and tears. Everyone wished to possess something that had belonged to her, something for "thoughts and remembrances;" something that might be guarded with the same devotion as the votive offering of a saint, or the relic of a martyr. She gave her shawl, her gloves, the feathers of her hat, which were cut into shreds, and distributed among her followers.

If history has bestowed the tribute of applause on Elizabeth at Tilbury-Fort, and on Maria Theresa at Buda, a splendid page is also reserved for the daughter of Louis XVI. at Bordeaux.

The royalist party in the western departments, of La Vendée and Brittany, flew to arms, and remained masters of the country they inhabited, but were not in sufficient force to march upon Paris. The want of combination rendered all these partial attempts unsuccessful; and the French, expecting little from intestine divisions, turned their eyes with confidence towards the north, and were earnest in calculating the march of the allies, from whom alone they hoped for their deliverance.

The courage of the adherents to the royal cause was strengthened by the king's proclamations from Ghent, and the accounts of the preparations of the allied armies, which were circulated among the public. These papers no sooner arrived in Paris than they were copied by ten thousand pens. The press also immediately groaned with these forbidden sheets, which were printed in defiance of all authority, and, during the night, pasted up in the streets in contempt of all danger.

The government meanwhile redoubled its efforts to raise the public mind to a proper degree of elevation; and perceiving that the intelligence received of the operations beyond the frontiers, had effectually belied the fable of the truce of twenty years, and the arrival of the empress and the child, felt that it behoved them to give no further countenance to these fictions. They, however, endeavoured to persuade the nation that these pretended hostilities were the work only of a faction headed by the Bourbons, and that no more danger was to be apprehended from their efforts, than had been felt from those of the first emigration.

The council of state, in its assembly of the 12th April, entered profoundly into this matter. Bonaparte, at a review in the court of the Tuileries, had, in the vehemence of his harangue to the troops, declared that, should the combined powers send against him six hundred thousand men, he would answer them by two millions. Shortly after, a levy of upwards of that number was ordered to take place throughout the whole of France, consisting of every man from the age of twenty to sixty. The council, finding it impossible to conceal from the public what passed beyond the frontiers, deemed it expedient to avow those impolitic transactions of the Congress, and to answer its declaration.

It was asserted by the French Government, that this declaration, supposed to have been made the 13th March, at Vienna, was apocryphal, and, for divers reasons, could not have emanated from the Congress, nor have been really signed by the ministers whose names appeared to give it sanction.

This declaration, known at Paris the preceding month, was now published throughout France, with the commentaries of the council, pronounced by them to be a forgery, and a fabrication of the agents of the Count of Lisle, (Louis XVIII.) and an incentive to assassination.

The object of the minister of police, by whom this answer was published, was probably to signify to the whole of France the determination of the Congress respecting Bonaparte, and this intelligence could not have been more dexterously or generally conveyed.

After thus establishing the falsehood of the declaration of Congress, a recapitulation was made of the various points in which the allied powers, and the Bourbons, had violated the treaty made with Bonaparte after his retreat to the isle of Elba, and which justified his return to France. A comparison was then drawn of the government under the administration of the Bourbons, and of its fatal consequences, not forgetting the tythes and the national domains, and the free government which was soon to take place under the benign protection of the laws and the emperor. This thrice-told tale of the wrongs of the Bourbons, and the rights of Bonaparte, which had already been published to satiety, was probably thought by the minister a necessary passport for the intelligence to the whole of the French nation, that the time allotted to Bonaparte to withdraw from France was expired, and that the allied armies were on their march towards the frontiers to enforce obedience.

This declaration seemed sufficient; but, as if the caprice of confession had seized the government, it was followed by a report of the minister of foreign affairs, in which he called the emperor's attention to the real perilous state of the country on account of the lawless conduct of the sovereigns of Europe, who were now in hostile array; who had arrested his messengers and refused to enter into any communication with him; that equal disrespect had been evinced towards the fraternal applications of his majesty to the sovereigns, though he had written to each, in his own hand, beginning with the endearing appellation of "*Monsieur, mon Frère.*" "Against whom," says the minister, "are those hostilities directed? Sire, it is your majesty that is named, but it is France that is threatened."

It had been well understood in Paris, that Bonaparte's presence in France was the sole cause of the impending calamities; but here was the solemn ministerial confession, published by order of the government. The whole fabric of falsehood was thus swept away by the hand that had raised it. Instead of the twenty years' truce, it was decreed that every citizen should arm in defence of the frontiers; and the devastation, if not the subjugation of the country, superseded all the fairy dreams of liberty, equality, and the rights of man.

Notwithstanding the official revelation of these dreadful truths, it was still thought expedient to keep up the semblance of concord and popularity at the Tuileries, although the council-chamber was often the arena of the bitterest contention. Many an angry discussion took place, but no one was so frequently called to order as the emperor himself. In the heat of debate he sometimes forgot that he was not emperor at home. But the execution of his threat of ordering a minister to be shot was adjourned by that minister's assurance, that the emperor himself would not survive an hour after.

These controversies in the cabinet of the Tuileries were not altogether unknown to the Parisians, and were even sometimes rehearsed before the mob, hired to cry "*Vive l'Empereur!*" Acclamations were at first purchased at the rate of five *livres* a day, but the price was now reduced; no effort of the lungs was paid higher than thirty or forty sous, and the enthusiasm of the populace diminished in proportion to its current value, and even their respect was measured by their salary. An animated discussion between Bonaparte and his arch-chancellor happening to take place at the window of his apartment in the Tuileries, the emperor, accustomed to ill-treat his ministers, seized him by the collar. This scene was witnessed by the mob, who related to their fellows the scuffle between Père la Violette and his comrade, in the same manner as they would have recounted one of the battles which takes place for their amusement, between the puppet-show actors, on the *boulevards*.

LETTER 7

May, 1815.

The veil is at length withdrawn; the comedy is ended; Bonaparte is no longer the humble candidate for public favour, the dependent on the protection of his ministers and council, the penitent convert from the errors of his former despotism:—he is once more Napoleon;— "*Napoleon, by the grace of God and the constitutions of the empire, &c. &c.*"

He has fled from the Tuileries, and entrenched himself at the Palais Bourbon, in the Champs Elysées, surrounded by his faithful *sicaires*, leaving the ideologues of his council to arrange what he calls their revolutionary rubbish, such as sovereign people, equal rights,. &c. with which they were active in forming a free constitution.

Few had been the dupes of Bonaparte's pretended conversion; but it was generally supposed that the consideration of the perilous situation in which he had placed himself, might have led him to act his part in this comedy of patriotism, till he was firmly seated on his throne by the assembly of the Field of May. He might then more easily seize the occasion of wielding unrestrained his old imperial sceptre.

What appeared most extraordinary to the Parisians was, not that Bonaparte should have acted the hypocrite; that on his landing he should have been the first to proclaim equal rights, equal laws; falsehood was known to be a constituent part of his character: his remaining a prisoner at the Tuileries, obliged to display himself daily at his windows, and return the salutations of the greasy mob, who were hired to vociferate "*Vive l'Empereur!*" and who, on the diminution of their pay, had changed their cry to "*Vive le Père la Violette!*" seemed unnecessary degradation. This humiliation, however, Napoleon might perhaps have borne, or dissembled; but to be forced to be present at the discussion of the council-chamber on the formation of a constitution, to find his observations treated with undue irreverence as foreign to the object of debate, to aid in forging the chains which he was destined to wear,—this was beyond all mortal patience.

That of Napoleon had long been exhausted, and he tore away the mask when the first favourable moment of emancipation presented itself. The council had decreed, that until the constitution in discussion had received the assent of the electors, the emperor should exercise his usual authority. Bonaparte availed himself of this decree. To be really emperor but for a day, an hour, was better than an eternity of bondage at the Tuileries. He therefore resorted once more to his old maxim of *daring*; and his imperial majesty, without taking leave, enthroned himself in full power, at the palace called the Elysée-Bourbon, in the Champs Elysées. Bonaparte lost few of his allies by this removal.

The soldiers, who had disdained to appear with the mob, and hail their emperor, while he was a prisoner at the Tuileries, accepted the fraternisation offered at the Champs Elysées, where the emperor returned their greetings at his leisure, from the gardens of his palace, and occasionally sent them a representative, which was usually one of his family.

The difficulties which would have attended the formation of a constitution suited for France, were at this moment greatly increased by an utter discordance in the views and interest of most of the persons employed in the fabrication. Those ministers, and members of the council, who had been accustomed to constitution-making, were of opinion that the French, as a free nation, should be furnished with a free constitution; that the sovereignty of the people might be exercised on the present occasion; and that on the convocation of the Field of May, the body of electors, as the immediate representatives of the people, should have the power of changing whatever disposition might be deemed by them unfavourable, and of adopting such measures as they should judge expedient for the interest of their country. Various were the plans for the organization of this crowd of special representatives, amounting to about twenty-five thousand electors. It was at length settled that committees should be named by the electors, from their own body, who should propose and discuss such changes, and whose reports should be made to the mass, distributed into sections, so that the opinion of the whole might be almost individually obtained.

But these organisers might have spared themselves the labour of such arrangements: Bonaparte had other projects; and having called to his aid a celebrated publicist, gained the start of the deliberating council at the Tuileries, and published, instead of a constitution, what he styled *An Additional Act to the Constitutions of the Empire*, dated from the palace of the Elysée, the 22nd April, 1815.

Bonaparte, notwithstanding the huzzas of the military and the mob, now found that not only his popularity was on the decline, but that even his partisans began to waver. All the hopes of those who had fondly imagined that a national contract was about to be formed which might cement the rights of the people, and limit the different powers; all these hopes vanished, when Bonaparte, by the sovereign authority vested in him by the constitutions of the empire, which he declared had been accepted by the people, ordered, for various reasons stated in the preamble, that the articles forming an additional act to these aforesaid constitutions, should also be submitted to the free and solemn acceptance of the citizens throughout the empire.

Had this string of articles resounded with national sovereignty, equality, and rights of man; and had the act conferred every kind of liberty, and made all republican concessions, the mode of its promulgation would too clearly have implied that it was merely an imperial mandate, which, like all others emanating from the same source, could serve only as an instrument to sanction all his past and future tricks of despotism.

The danger of a deliberating mass of twenty to thirty thousand citizens was too obvious to escape Bonaparte's penetration; but as it had been decreed that the assembly of the Champ de Mars should take place, it was impossible to countermand the meeting; measures were, however, taken to neutralize its effect. The electors were to receive no pecuniary compensation for their expenses of travelling, or residence in Paris, which was a circumstance favourable to Bonaparte, since no great number were disposed to undertake the journey at their own cost; and it was intimated to those whom patriotic sentiments, and the hope of co-operating in the establishment of a free constitution might prompt to such an effort, that, by an imperial decree, the electors were not to discuss the Constitutional Act, and that their services would be limited to verifying the registers, and counting the votes on the day of their meeting in the Field of May, which was to be held on the 26th of that month.

The operations of the electors were, of course, reduced to the service of clerks, since assent or disapprobation of the Constitutional Act was no more their concern. The same decree enacted the mode of taking those votes on registers opened at the town-houses, at the offices of government, and at notaries, where the votes were inscribed. This mode of voting had its precedent in the mockery of Bonaparte's election as emperor; and it was presumed that the same nefarious manoeuvres would be resorted to; but as that election was chiefly confined to Paris, where not only the boasted four millions of signatures, but ten millions might have been obtained with equal facility, by similar means, it was feared that the agents of government in the departments would construe the title of active citizens in too confined a sense, and admit none to vote but such as had the civic right.

To avert the inconvenience that might arise from too formal an adherence to the letter of the decree, and lest those in office might harbour some lurking attachment to the cause of the Bourbons, or retain some anti-imperial prejudices, it was ordered by Bonaparte that certain good and trusty commissaries should be sent into each military division to expel from office all mayors, municipal officers, members of general councils of departments, sub-*prefects*, and others bearing authority, and name other sound and trusty men in their place.

These commissaries sped away from Paris to execute their revolutionary orders, and raise the spirit of the departments to a proper sense of the new imperial condescension of submitting any act whatever to their consideration or choice.

This mode of enlightening the departments was judged the more expedient, as the Constitutional Act emanated from the Elysée palace had undergone the sarcasms and reproach of all classes at Paris. The Jacobins, who had triumphed in imperial conversion, and who attributed this patriotic change to the conviction of the truth of their system, now lavished on Bonaparte all the disgraceful and ill-sounding epithets which filled the pages of their vocabulary. The republican party had given very little credit to any conversion whatever; they had felt that the sacrifice to principle would be great in placing Bonaparte as chief of the executive power, although bound by fetters which they hoped to rivet on him; but they had believed that, in the present crisis of his fate, he might be led to risk some portion of his power to ensure the rest, and that he might, in the perilous circumstances in which he was placed, suffer his interest to outweigh his vanity.

The royalists alone felt a species of triumph at this patriotic disappointment. Their hopes were fixed on the frontiers; and they concluded that this rage for constitution-making would be abated by the same means that would reconcile many other differences. All classes, however discordant in every other opinion, were now in unison on one point, that Bonaparte was the most daring of impostors. All were unprepared for this state-mockery, and it filled their minds with uncontrollable indignation. Was it not enough, said they, to delude us with the tale of a twenty years' truce, and the arrival of his wife and child, as proofs of his new alliance with one of the most formidable of our enemies; was it not enough that he has brought war and devastation upon us, by a second invasion of all the powers of Europe, who will not fail to pour on us all the stores of their vengeance, and punish us as slaves in revolt? Could he even frame an excuse or justification of these falsehoods, and plead that he had deceived us, because he had been himself deceived, this deception at least, which he now practises, is an act of his own will.

He had adopted principles, which are recognised by the nation; he assented to a constitution framed on those principles, and for the formation of which he convoked the country in the persons of its immediate representatives, to discuss and sanction what should be proposed by his ministers and council; and then, after declaring that the people had approved the various acts of despotism which he and the senate had promulgated at different periods of his tyranny, he enacts, of his own authority, another constitution, which he calls on the nation to fall down, and worship.

These murmurs were so general, that the emperor thought them entitled to some notice; finding a spirit of resistance arising against this second treachery, he deemed it proper to allege something in his defence. This defence consisted chiefly in recrimination. Bonaparte's despotism had been founded on the knowledge he had of the national character, of which the leading feature is vanity, and which had been flattered by the appellation of the Great Nation, which was the result of his military achievements. He now reproached them with their abject meanness by which they had received a constitution without a murmur, which the king had *octroyed* to them as a boon; which he had sent to the municipalities, not to be accepted, but obeyed, and in the preamble of which he declared himself to be in full possession of the authority emanated from God, and from his ancestors. Bonaparte compared the French of the present day to the serfs who were freed by one of their former monarchs, Louis le Gros.

Bonaparte had forgotten that, although his own *senatus consulta* had not been "*octroyed*," but accepted by the people, they had, in reality, as little to do in their formation as the senate itself, who simply registered the imperial dictate, and often bore with impatience the indignities to which they were compelled to submit.

LETTER 8

June, 1815.

It has been said by the moralist, "*never be such a fool as to be a knave;*" but the policy of Napoleon soared far beyond the trite and vulgar maxims of moral conduct. His principles respecting government, and his own actions, whether public or private, were regulated by no other views than those of his own immediate interests. He had chosen Machiavel for his guide, and applied the politics, maxims, and practices of the Italian states, to our own enlightened times, and to France, which having subdued, he attempted to make his instrument of the subjection of Europe.

His previous studies had led him to believe that not only the territory of France was his property, but its inhabitants also; he spoke often, with the triumph of a wealthy prodigal, of his ability of spending twenty and thirty thousand men each month; and made no more account of this sort of expenditure, than of the millions of gold and silver which he exacted and lavished. His most ardent ambition was that of living in history, provided that it was not such a writer as Tacitus who should convey his name to posterity, and for whom he affected the most profound contempt. In a discussion with the historic class of the Institute, he asserted that Tacitus was the most partial, misinformed, and ill-advised of all historians; and that he had libelled a model of wisdom among the Roman emperors, Tiberius, of whose policy in government he had not the sagacity to form a just opinion. The Institute was compelled to leave Tacitus to defend himself, and Tiberius to the honours of his new reputation.

Bonaparte had signalised himself as a warrior, but he did not too highly deem of descending to posterity with military fame alone. He had observed that nothing of the most celebrated destroyers of mankind, called warriors, exists but their names; while its great institutors are not merely held in remembrance, but continue to live in their disciples; all that remained of Alexander, of Caesar, of Charles XII. was their names; but the laws instituted more than four thousand years since by Moses, were yet obeyed throughout the world, by the numerous and disseminated posterity of his race;—that Zoroaster and Mahomet had subdued, by their principles, a great portion of the earth, and that their names are still invoked with veneration by innumerable followers; while the heroes of Greece and Rome fade on the memory; that, in modern times, Luther and Calvin had given their names to the most enlightened portion of the people of Europe; and that he also, Napoleon the Great, by seizing some favourable *epocha* for a new kind of warfare against all that he called superstition, might become the founder of some other system of faith, and assume the honours of a teacher or a prophet.

Bonaparte had not only meditated on this subject, but had made reformation the secret order of the day, in a committee of his council of state. Without having plunged deeply into religious controversy, or having probably carried his studies beyond the lucubrations of modern infidelity, he had the sagacity to discern that the prevalent religion of his empire held little relation with the primitive doctrines Christianity, and that the state of knowledge in France was such that reformation would be welcomed. Orders were given at the literary police to permit the publication of all works against popery; and coercive measures were in meditation against the person of the Pope, who had resisted his anti-canonical measures respecting the institution of bishops. This was a power which interfered too much with his own, and he wished to annex the title of Head of the Church to that of Emperor of the French.

Bonaparte had distinguished himself at all times for his principles of toleration, which benefited only the dissenters from the Catholic church. These were favoured; while the Episcopal chiefs of the church avoided any open hostilities, only by becoming the instruments of his edicts of conscription, or flatterers of his power. Their charges, or *mandemens*, to the clergy and people of their dioceses, were filled with scriptural allusions to Cyrus; and one bishop so far forgot his allegiance to the Pope as to name Bonaparte the representative of God on earth. The clergy of inferior rank, whose salaries were by no means adequate to their services, or who had clearer views of Bonaparte's ultimate designs, were unwilling to compliment away their faith, and made scriptural allusions, in their turn, in answer to the *mandemens* of their bishops.

History teaches us that arbitrary power and the sword are not always unfitted to promote a reform of ancient errors. Mahomet proposed the great doctrine of the Unity of the Divine Being, and purified the Christian, and what yet remained of the heathen world, of its polytheistic and idolatrous abuses; and Henry VIII. shook off with violence the chains of the papal government. Of these two creeds, a warlike nation of the east, the Mahometan. Wechabites, appear to have undertaken a further reform. The papal superstition would not, perhaps, have survived Bonaparte's examination. He had found too many points of opposition in the tenets of this church to fashion it to his rule of government, and bring it within the pale of his system of unity. He had, indeed, observed in Egypt the policy of ancient Rome in adopting the religion of the conquered country. He says to the chief priests of Cairo:

Glory to *Allah!* There is no other God, but God; Mahomet is his prophet, and I am his friend. The divine *Koran* is the delight of my soul, and the object of my meditation.

A discussion which he held with those eastern doctors led to some doubts respecting the strength of faith in their proselyte. Bonaparte would not admit that the magnetical needle, the invention of gunpowder, the art of printing, or the Newtonian system of the universe, were to be found in the Koran. But whatever might be the doctrines which Bonaparte would have instituted, and for the belief of which all latitude would have been given, the discipline of his church would no doubt have been military. He had already rendered the instruction at the Lyceums, and even private schools, as soldier-like as the nature of the lessons permitted, and every movement was ordered by beat of drum. A right reverend bench of generals, well organised staffs of deans and vicars, and a handsomely drilled clergy, with their acolytes, would, in his estimation, have given energy to the church-militant. As a sedentary guard, or militia, they would have replaced the regular troops stationed in the interior, and with which he could have augmented his ranks for foreign service.

The teachers of virtue might thus have become the quellers of sedition, and their eloquent discourses against immorality be accompanied, if necessary, by the stronger arguments of military persuasion. As his system had been that of fusion in his secular concerns, so he would have followed the same rule in his ecclesiastical administration, and this he would have called toleration. He had not been able, however, to bring the Pope, when in Paris, into union with the president of the Protestant church, M. Marron, whom he usually addressed at court by the title of *"Monsieur le Pape Protestant."* Pius VII. declared, with some pleasantry, that he had no hopes *"de tirer le Maron du feu."* But Napoleon effected what was no less difficult, that of engaging the Cardinal Archbishop of Paris, and the Protestant president, to join in the same religious ceremony, in the presence of the empress, and part of the court. It was the celebration of the marriage of a Catholic and a Protestant person of the court; and the man being a Protestant, the Protestant president, in right of the husband's prerogative, took the lead in the ceremony, and was seated in the place of honour, at the right hand of the empress, at the nuptial banquet, and the cardinal was placed on the left.

It is soothing to observe that toleration in France is not confined to courts, much less did it belong exclusively to his reign, who, in his complete indifference for all religion, was a Mussulman at Cairo, and a Catholic at Paris. Louis XVIII. while he adheres with steadfast attachment to that religion in which he so long found the solace of his misfortunes, and of which the consolations consolations blunt the thorns that surround his diadem, Louis XVIII. has never violated the sacred principle of toleration. In testimony of the truth of this assertion, I shall mention the circumstances which took place last winter at an interment some leagues distant from Paris, and at which the President of the Protestant church was invited to officiate. The defunct was a titled English Protestant.

The bishop of the diocese had ordered that all due honours should be rendered to the piety and good works of the deceased. The funeral sermon was preached by the Protestant president, in the pulpit of a Catholic church, to a numerous Catholic auditory, the Catholic clergy attending the service. The corpse was laid in the tomb with mingled rites; the lighted tapers, and the Catholic dirge, the prayers of the Genevan church, and the tears of the mourning peasantry. You have heard of the object of this blended ceremonial. She was an English lady of some renown about the middle of the last century. Her misfortunes, and her errors, (for which the tears that were shed by the poor over her grave are a proof she had atoned,) have been recorded by the celebrated Junius under the name of Miss Ann, or Nancy Parsons.

Bonaparte was well read in the history of the doubtful authority and genealogy of the papal doctrine; and a counsellor of state, whom he had entrusted with the project, told me that the emperor was persuaded, that the doctors of the Gallican church would be flexible enough[4] to swell the number of their four articles of dissent from papal pretension.

Having found that the Pope had become less complaisant than when he was his guest at the Tuileries, he began the execution of his design by putting the Holy Father in durance, and constituting him prisoner in one of the French departments. The intervention of some pressing business, either the projected invasion of England, or a predatory expedition on the continent, and which required his presence, interrupted the plan of being the instructor of mankind, and he reassumed his ordinary occupation of being its scourge. In this career he had, at that period, much yet to perform. A new religion could be established, when he thought proper, by a *senatus consultus*; and in the meantime he had sacrifices to make to his household gods of the fam-

---

4. The decrees which he enforced with the most unrelenting severity were those of the conscription. Strict obedience to this murderous mandate was enjoined in the pastoral letters of bishops to their dioceses. A certain archbishop enforced his argument in favour of this depopulating decree by asserting that Jesus Christ had submitted himself to the conscription. It was thus that the Reverend Father in God translated, by the word conscription, the inscription, or taxation, which took place by order of Augustus when Cyrenius was Governor of Syria, and "*when Joseph went up to Bethlehem, with Mary, to be taxed, being great with child.*" This prelate's zeal for his majesty's service would have enlarged the conscription to females, and infants yet unborn, while the French emperor's mandate went no farther than the male sex, and those at the age of eighteen, when they were inhumanly called, "*chair à canon*"—"food for powder."

ily of Teutates. But leaving him to accomplish his great resolve,

> *On Moscow's towers let Gallic standards fly,*
> *And all be mine beneath the polar sky,*

. . . .let us return to the sketch of his later adventures.

It was now clearly understood that the loan of a new constitution must be repaid by the sacrifice of the lives and fortunes of all the citizens of France. But as few of this number admitted the value of this loan, or were disposed to make the return exacted, Bonaparte had not been negligent in seeking aid from without. Considerable expectations were raised on the diversion to be made by his brother, the King of Naples, who, under pretence of giving independence and freedom to Italy, had marched a very numerous and well appointed army to the northern states of that Peninsula, which, in the congressional repartition of European souls, had been attached to the House of Austria.

It was no doubt generous in this king, at the time when the other princes of Europe were carving out countries for themselves, and each other, to volunteer his services in the obsolete cause of the rights of man, and of the independence of nations. He had succeeded in sending the Pope again on his travels, to the great satisfaction of the Romans; but not satisfied with this easy conquest, when Murat attempted to cope with the Austrian armies, which, in their march towards France, had stopped to reconnoitre his proceedings, he was vanquished in several successive engagements, compelled to seek his safety in flight, and learnt, on his arrival on the French shore, that his kingdom was departed from him.

The loss or gain of a crown, in this age of revolutions, excites no great interest, except with the gaining or losing parties. This incident was not, however, unimportant to Europe, since it procured a very considerable additional force to the cause of the allied armies. Murat was naturally regarded by the august members of the European family as unworthy of his station, and fit only to be cast out; while Bonaparte considered him as guilty, because he had been unfortunate, although Murat, who had lost his crown by listening to his seductions, might well have answered,

> *Faults I may have to Heaven, but none to thee.*

Murat had borne his faculties at Naples as meekly as could have been expected from the possessor of a throne so equivocal. He had obtained the good opinion of the country in general, whose well-being he seemed to have at heart, and which he had, in various instances, effected. It was hoped that this part of Europe, which had been stained with no ordinary crimes under its old masters, might regain its former prosperity under a milder administration, and that the multiplied depredations made on the property of the noble and the rich might be, in a great measure, retrieved.

All this was promised by the king, and was believed by those who had suffered most under Sicilian and Bonapartean rulers. The Neapolitans were not reserved in the expression of their satisfaction, and appeared to dread no interruption of their tranquillity, but such as might arise from the arbiters of the fate of nations at the Congress; though they hoped that the conduct of Murat in the great campaign of Europe, 1814, and the treaties formed with him by the leading powers, would determine that sovereign body to treat him with favour.

But while the Neapolitans, many of whom are personally known to me, were expressing their apprehensions respecting the final decisions of the Congress, there was an enemy almost at their gates, who, in the vast overthrow of crowned heads which he was planning in his little island, had comprehended that of the King of Naples. Though Murat might have made a tolerably decent kind of king, he was endowed with no extraordinary intelligence. He had indeed, prepared for defence, if he were attacked; his army was respectable, and might have contributed to the preservation of his sovereignty, had he continued to act the part which he adopted the last year, and joined his forces with the rest of Europe against its common disturber.

But in evil hour, he listened to the wily seducer, who, meditating his march from his place of exile to Paris, persuaded this foolish king, that the active employment of his troops against their common enemies was the most effectual method of not only securing the possession of his own crown, but of rendering Italy independent. Murat's expedition against the Austrians ended as might reasonably be supposed, against forces so superior. The liberties and independence of Italy were not to be assured by measures so inadequate. The Italians were too wary to confide their destinies to a general like Murat, or to such a protector of national independence as Bonaparte.

All hopes of external alliance had now vanished; and Austria, instead of coming to Napoleon's aid, as he had pretended, having crushed his brother-in-law, who was active in his cause, he was left to his own resources and to his allies the military, and the *sansculotterie* or *canaille* of Paris. Since the appearance of his Constitutions, the fervour

52

of this last body of active citizens had, however, been considerably abated. Some, who considered him as an apostate from the faith, were become very lukewarm in their alliance; others, as the subsidies had ceased, misspent their time no longer in vociferation. This turbulent class did not return to their accustomed labour, for all workshops were shut up, as all commerce was at an end. Their residence in Paris was dangerous, and required the strict surveillance of the national guard. A few were engaged by the government to work at the fortifications round Paris, and others engaged themselves as members of the *Corps Francs* to guard the country round the metropolis.

The *Corps Francs* were organised bands of volunteers, hired by some chief, commissioned by the police. They had been instituted in the last campaign to protect the rural communes of the departments round Paris from pillage by the scattered Russian Cossacks. The daily papers were filled with doleful accounts of depredation and violence committed by these northern barbarians. All the horrors of war were poured on the inhabitants, and files of municipal certificates were published, with the intention of rousing the citizens of Paris to resistance, lest such also should be their fate.

This part of the business was ill managed, for it was proved that no Russian Cossacks had entered these departments; and that all these horrors had been committed by the volunteers of the *Corps Francs*, or, as they were called, the Cossacks of the Fauxbourgs St. Antoine and St. Marceau, who had assumed the costume of the Russian Cossacks. In a village on the Marne, near Meaux, in the direction of which the allied armies were expected, a Russian general, Rusky Musky, or by some such name was he called, had given orders to his little advanced army of Cossacks to levy contributions, and take with them the furniture of the houses in which he had fixed his quarters. Intelligence of this was conveyed to the proprietor of a villa, and who was a colonel stationed with his regiment of regular troops at Meaux.

He advanced privately to reconnoitre the enemy; he admired the dexterity with which he saw his property packed up and placed on Russian conveyances. He brought up his regiment, surrounded his house, and made General Rusky Musky and all his troops prisoners of war. Soon after, each man of this little Russian army was strung up by the neck on the trees which formed the avenue leading to his house. The general was convicted of being the upholsterer in the Fauxbourg St. Antoine, who had furnished the house the preceding year, and his army was composed of the workmen of that quarter of Paris.

Such were part of the measures then taken by Bonaparte's police to excite the country and Paris to useless resistance against the invading armies. The Cossacks of the north were less dreaded than the Cossacks of Paris. The former, though authorised plunderers, were often found capable of lenient measures, and sometimes even of sentiment, a proof of which took place in the environs of Fontainebleau, with which I shall close this rambling letter.

A Polish regiment, forming part of the advanced guard of the Russian Army, after expelling the French from Troyes, marched upon Fontainebleau. The troops were foraging in a neighbouring village, and were about to commit disorders, which would have caused considerable loss to the proprietors, without benefit to themselves; such as piercing the banks, or forcing the sluices of some fish-ponds. While they were thus employed, and their officers Looking on, they were astonished to hear the word of command bidding them to cease, pronounced in their own language, by a person in the dress of the upper class of peasants. They ceased their attempt at further spoliation, and drew near the stranger. He represented to the troops the useless mischief they were about to commit, and ordered them to withdraw. The officers coming up were lectured in their turn; and heard with the same astonishment the laws of predatory warfare explained to them:

When I had a command in the army, of which your regiment is a part, I punished very severely such acts as you seem to authorise by your presence; and it is not on those soldiers but on you that punishment would have fallen.

To be thus tutored by a French farmer, in their own language, in such circumstances, and in such terms, was almost past endurance. They beheld the peasants at the same time taking off their hats, and surrounding the speaker, as if to protect him in case of violence; while the oldest among their own soldiers, anxiously gazing on the features of the stranger, were seized with a kind of involuntary trembling. Conjured more peremptorily, though respectfully, to disclose his quality and his name, the peasant, drawing his hand across his eyes to wipe off a starting tear, exclaimed, with an half stifled voice, "I am Kosciusko!"

The movement was electric. The soldiers threw down their arms, and falling prostrate on the ground, according to the custom of their country, covered their heads with sand. It was the prostration of the heart. On Kosciusko's return to his house in the neighbourhood of this scene, he found a Russian military post established to protect it.

The Emperor Alexander, having learnt from M. de la Harpe that Kosciusko resided in the country, ordered for him a guard of honour, and the country around his dwelling escaped all plunder and contribution.

Kosciusko had withdrawn some years since from the guilty world of Bonaparte to cultivate a little farm, rejecting every offer which was made him by Napoleon, who had learnt to appreciate his worth. Kosciusko knew him well. I called on him one day to bid him farewell, having read in the official paper of the morning his address to the Poles on the subject of recovering their freedom, being named to the command of the Polish army by Bonaparte. Kosciusko heard me with a smile at my credulity; but on my shewing him the address with his signature, he exclaimed:

This is all a forgery; Bonaparte knew me too well to insult me with any offer in this predatory expedition; he has adopted this mode, which I can neither answer nor resent, and which he attempts to colour with the pretext of liberty. His notions and mine respecting Poland are at as great a distance as our sentiments on every other subject.

Letter 9

June, 1815.

Bonaparte, on the failure of his ally, Murat, was now left to his own resources. Although he was proclaimed Emperor of the French by the complaisance of his council of state, and for which he had played so foully, he felt that his title even was precarious till it was confirmed by the assembled nation in the Field of May. It is not easy to conceive what could have engaged him to revive the remembrance of this feudal assembly of ancient French history, where the monarch met to deliberate with the great vassals of the crown, and the dignified clergy, on the urgent concerns of the state. At those early *epochas*, the Field of May might, with great propriety, be called the assembly of the nation; for as the property of the lands in the kingdom was almost wholly in the hands of those great personages who were called together on these occasions, they might be said to represent the nation; the rest, except a few small proprietors and inhabitants of towns, being composed of serfs attached to the soil.

Bonaparte knew, however, that this denomination of the Field of May was calculated to please his subjects by awakening their curiosity.

"What is the Field of May?" exclaimed the Parisians; at once something antique, and something new; where much was to be done for their liberties, and, what was not indifferent, an unknown ceremonial would be performed for their amusement. It may be observed, that one effect of twenty-five years' of revolution is to have given the French such restless habits, that they require continually something new or strange to occupy their minds, and fill up the void of ordinary life. When it *"keeps the noiseless tenor of its way,"* it appears to them a dull dead calm, in which the mind becomes stagnant.

It was much in favour of Bonaparte, that, during his reign, he had always something new to present for the entertainment of the Parisians; the bulletin of a battle, a victory, the entry into the great capitals of the north, something, as Bayes expresses it, to "surprise and elevate." The calm tranquillity which had prevailed during the ten months that Louis XVIII. had held the sceptre, although brightening into hope, and promising prosperity, might indeed be called happy, but was felt to be dull. In short, all Paris flocked in multitudes to see what was to be seen at the Field of May.

The Field of May having been recorded in history as a day of national meeting, the French were at least acquainted with the name; but as the invitation was now given to such as in former times would have been regarded as slaves, and serfs, Bonaparte had explained the nature of the business by decreeing from Lyons, that it was to be held for the formation of a free constitution, on the basis of the original principles of the revolution.

The electors, who had hastened from the departments to Paris to be present at this great solemnity, towards the end of the month, found that this Field of May was delayed till June; and also that their high destination of framing constitutions had been converted into an affair of arithmetic; and that all that was required of them was sufficient skill in addition, to cast up the votes of their constituents. Bonaparte had spared them all other patriotic labours, by enacting himself the constitution which he deemed the best fitted for them to obey.

The greater number therefore of the electors, finding that no discussions or changes were to be admitted, and that they were themselves objects of imperial contempt, unwilling to become the tame witnesses of this idle pageantry, returned indignantly to their homes, without waiting the holding of this mock assembly. Some less occupied, or more curious, forming about a tenth part of the whole body of the electors convoked, whiled away their time at Paris, till the day appointed for the assembly, which was held the beginning of June.

A spacious temporary amphitheatre had been erected for this purpose in the Champ de Mars, connected with the facade of the Military School, and containing about fifteen thousand persons, seated, and covered by an awning; these were the electors, and the military deputations. The sloping banks which arise round the Champ de Mars, were crowded with people, and its immense plain was filled with cavalry. Here an altar was placed, opposite the throne, which was erected within the amphitheatre. An assembly, composed of the electors remaining at Paris, had been held the day preceding that of the *Champ de Mai*, to hear the result of the registers for and against Napoleon's Additional Act; the votes were already enumerated by the clerks of the minister of the interior, and the only co-operation of the electors, and by which a judgment may be formed of their quality, was that of loud acclamations, each time the ministerial president's secretary declared the number of votes from a department, in favour of Napoleon. He had always boasted that he had been elected emperor by above four millions of votes.

The truth of this assertion was never ascertained; but whatever the numbers were, the measures taken to procure them vitiated the whole; not only as the validity of the votes was not scrutinized, but as the only qualification requisite was that of being sufficiently learned to write a name, which, whether real or fictitious, was of no import, since it was not examined.

As there was therefore no scrutiny, and the interest of the register-holder was to procure the greatest number of votes possible, the voting for the constitution was as defective as that for the emperorship. Although much manoeuvring was exercised by Bonaparte's special agents in the departments, such as changing the constituted authorities, mayors, sub-*prefects*, and others whose opinions were not sufficiently pronounced in favour of Napoleon's constitution, or who might have qualmish feelings respecting their oath to the Constitutional Chart of Louis XVIII. the number of votes declared at the assembly amounted only to one-fourth of the numbers that had been announced for the title of emperor. As this imperial edict, called Additional Act to the constitution already existing, was deemed to be accepted, the emperor, in his speech from the throne, assured the audience, which was of a very mixed quality, from the absence of many electors, and the necessity of filling the amphitheatre, that as "emperor, consul, and soldier, he held all from the people; and, like the king of Athens, would sacrifice himself for his country." A much less sacrifice was required by the oracle which had pronounced on his fate at Vienna, than from the king of Athens, whose patriotic sacrifice he was in no humour to imitate.

Napoleon arrived at the Champ de Mars at one o'clock, accompanied by his three brothers, Joseph, Lucien, and Jerome. These principal performers in this pageant appeared upon the foreground of the piece, detached from the surrounding figures by their Roman costumes; the tunic, over which was flung the large *manteau*, falling in ample folds. The ceremony began with high mass, after which followed a speech from the deputy appointed to harangue the emperor, and which he pronounced standing on one of the steps of the throne. Then came the declaration of the arch-chancellor, that the new Chart was accepted by an almost unanimity of votes. This was succeeded by a discourse of the emperor, after which he signed the Additional Act, to which he swore, upon the Evangelists, to adhere.

It may be observed, that Napoleon kept on his hat during the whole solemnity, before the assembled representatives of the nation, whose heads were uncovered; and even when he took the oath, as if to shew a sort of defiance of earth and of heaven. But in all probability it was from prudence that he kept on his hat, which was always lined with steel, and fitted to guard his head from danger. For the rest of his body he had nothing to fear, being always wrapped in a coat of mail. After having taken the oath, Napoleon descended from his throne, threw aside his *manteau*, and advancing towards the middle of the Champ de Mars, distributed his eagles to the troops of the line, and the national guard as they passed before him, and swore to defend their colours.

The air was then filled with the sounds ten thousand times repeated, of "*Vous jurez*," and "*Nous jurons!*" The ceremony being ended, the people returned to their homes, having found out what was meant by the Field of May; but somewhat discontented, that the most diverting part of the spectacle, the splendid firework they had been promised in the evening, representing the Isle of Elba, and many other curious and astonishing things, were deferred till the following Sunday, when the emperor was to go in state to the hall of the Legislative Body, and to open their sittings by a speech from the throne.

Thus ended the assembly of the Field of May, which had been contrived in order to deceive the nation; a purpose that was altogether unfulfilled, since nobody was deceived. Some friends of Bonaparte, or rather friends of their country, had, indeed, in privy councils, whispered in his ear, that he might convert the pageantry of the Field of May into a scene of real glory; that he had an act of noble magnanimity to perform; and this was, to sign voluntarily, in the presence of the assembled empire, his own abdication. He was reminded that all Europe was at his frontiers; that its tremendous coalition might be at first resisted, but must eventually subdue; and that his crown and person would be the price of peace. He was called upon by every motive that could be urged, to do what, in truth, was only an act of prudent foresight; but which, all present and future times would applaud, as the generous resolve of a great and lofty spirit. He had but to declare, that seeing he was made the pretext of the cruel invasion with which France was menaced, he relinquished the empire he had regained, and withdrew, in the hope of being followed by the good wishes of the nation, and perhaps of deserving its applause.

Had Bonaparte been capable of such voluntary descent, this would indeed have proved for him a proud day, of new and virtuous renown. The merit of the sacrifice would have been ad mitted to be proportionate to its greatness; and amidst all the horrors of his devastating ambition, this last scene of his public existence would have shone like a track of unsullied light, along a dark and stormy horizon.

But to return.—On the Sunday which followed the ceremony of the Field of May, the emperor went in his state-carriage, attended by the ladies of his dynasty, and preceded and followed by his numerous guards, in high military pomp, to install the legislature. He made his speech, in which he talked of independence, the rights of the people, the liberty of the press, and withdrew.

The evening of this day closed with illuminations, and the expected pyrotechnic exhibition, which represented Bonaparte in a ship, landing from the Isle of Elba, on the shores of Provence, and about to re-conquer France. The firework was one of the best-acted scenes in this great comedy; it amused the Parisians, which "*is what they most seek*" in Revolutions. The mob cried, "Long live the Emperor and fireworks!" and the reign of the Constitutional Monarchy began.

Meanwhile, the more reflecting citizens of Paris mourned over the evils which menaced their unhappy country. The armies of Europe already begirted its frontiers, and the miseries of civil war desolated its western coasts. Napoleon, however reluctant to depart, saw the necessity of joining his army, and only waited to receive the address of the legislature, in answer to his imperial speech at the opening of the session. The framing of this answer presented so many difficulties, so many apprehensions of saying too little, or too much, that new models were formed, and rejected, during several days, before a choice was made.

The first act of the Chamber of Representatives was the nomination of M. Lanjuinais as president. This choice looked like independence, since they could scarcely have made an election less agreeable to Napoleon. M. Lanjuinais, during his perilous revolutionary career, had acquired the esteem of all parties. His aversion to Bonaparte had never been dissembled. When Napoleon's faction first raised him to the emperorship, M. Lanjuinais, then a member of the Senate, rebuked the servility of his colleagues, in full assembly.

"What!" exclaimed he, "will you submit to give your country a master taken from a race, of origin so ignominious, that the Romans disdained to employ them as slaves?"

Several acts of irreverence had widened the breach, and it was expected, that this nomination would not receive the imperial sanction. But as Napoleon's interest led him, at this moment, not to be on ill terms with the legislature, he dissembled his resentment, and acceded to the choice. He was less reserved, however, with the Legislative Body itself, when at length they presented their address, says he:

> You may meditate on the constitution I have given you; you may prepare organic regulations; but beware, touch not the ark itself; you know the danger that awaits such profanation.—My ministers will tell you the rest.

Having placed this monument under the guardianship of his Houses of Commons, and of Peers, which he had also named, Bonaparte prepared himself to enter the field against the presumptuous foes that were about to invade his frontiers.

He did not dissemble that the glory of the Duke of Wellington had sometimes a little eclipsed his own. He had often, in conversation, told his marshals, that Wellington was the second general in Europe; but he had learnt, during his retreat, that the palm of generalship had been contested, and that there were gainsayers perverse enough to doubt the justice of the rank he had conferred on himself.—He said, rubbing his hands:

> Well, I have never had the good fortune to come across him; *Je vais me frottr contre* Wellington, and I shall send you a good account of him.

With this presentiment he set off for the north, exultingly, *"pour se frotter contre* Wellington."

M. Carnot, in his report on the military state of the empire, had raised the troops of the line to half a million; and the numerical amount of the army to eight hundred and fifty thousand men. This statement was greatly exaggerated; for M. Carnot either counted as being really under arms, the number of men exacted from each department, or, the lists sent up by the prefects of the number that had marched from the different districts, or *arrondissemens*. As minister of the interior, he might have some grounds for this assertion; but as a soldier, he was guilty of misstatement; for he could not be ignorant that the citizen, or peasant, who had no means of resisting power, in their insulated dwellings, having obeyed the injunction of the *prefect*, or his subordinate authorities, to march from home, deemed it unnecessary to make further advances than the boundaries of their departments, and that the greater number found means to wheel to the right, or the left, and turning from the frontier, march back to their respective homes.

The first division of four thousand of those volunteers, that had marched from Paris, escorted by the *gendarmerie*, for Nancy, were met halfway near Verdun, diminished to five hundred and thirty: the leader asserting to the person who told me, that he did not expect to reach Nancy with more than his own company of *gendarmes*.

The minister must have been informed of these defections in the supernumerary two millions of men, which Bonaparte had retorted on the allied powers, when they menaced to send a million to dispossess him of his throne. M. Carnot's report on the state of France was so much the more grateful to the ear of Napoleon, as he had not only exaggerated the military force, but had often overstepped the modesty of official detail, by courtier-like strokes of the vast superiority of Napoleon's administration over that of the Bourbons. This report consisted of eighteen sections, such as those of Commerce, Manufactures, Marine, Finance, &c. &c.; in each of which the conduct of the king and the emperor was contrasted, and always in favour of the latter. For instance, in the section on the Imperial Guard, The minister says:

Europe is acquainted with the courage, the *sangfroid*, the fidelity of this guard, an unassailable rampart during war, and the ornament of the capital in time of peace; this noble corps were treated by the Bourbons with hatred and contempt.

The hatred for these *Praetorian* bands was not confined to the

Bourbons; they were objects of jealousy to the great mass of the army, on account of the distinctions conferred on them by Bonaparte, and of their superiority of pay; and of terror to the citizens in general, who considered them as the rampart of imperial despotism. The minister says:

> The acclamations which welcomed the emperor on his return among the French, have led him to judge that such a people may be entrusted to govern themselves, and he has therefore given them the liberty of the press.

Was M. Carnot the only person in Paris ignorant from what lips issued these acclamations, and the daily price paid *pour aller au cri?* which was the familiar term used by those who were hired to vociferate, "*Vive l'Empereur!*" under the windows of his apartment at the Tuileries. Some persons, who pretend to have been in the secret of what passed in Napoleon's retirement at the Elysée, assert, that this report on the state of the nation, which it was considered as highly important to render flattering to the public eye, was not the report of the minister to the emperor, but that of the emperor to the minister.

LETTER 10

June, 1815.

Bonaparte, having expedited all his civil affairs, such as the installation of his Chambers of Commons, and of Peers, informed them that his first duty called him to meet the formidable coalition of emperors and kings that threatened their independence, and that the army and himself would acquit themselves well; recommending to them the destinies of France, with his own personal safety, and above all, the liberty of the press.

When all the ceremonials were completed, Bonaparte, smiling within himself at his re-shackled slaves, set off for the frontiers. The prize which was now to be contested was of no ordinary worth; the leaders who were about to meet his hostile garb bore names of no vulgar renown, and the world hung in dread attention on the deep tragedy which was about to be represented. The allied armies were now drawing nearer on every side, and war was inevitable; notwithstanding the continued imperial declarations to the last that affairs would be amicably arranged, and that some parts of the frontiers near the southeast were actually invaded: but as the armies the most dreaded were those hanging on the northern frontier, particularly that under English orders, it was against this part of the allies that every possible force was directed. It was concluded that the overthrow of this army, of which no doubt could be admitted, so immense were the preparations against it, would strike a salutary terror into the forces of the other coalised powers, and, determine them to a revision of their late precipitate and ill-advised treaties.

Every exertion was therefore made to assemble such an army as should merit the name of invincible. The choicest troops of the various armies, with a most numerous, and well stored *matériel*, headed by the emperor, had raised the hopes of the Bonapartists to the highest pitch of enthusiasm, and with whom no doubt was entertained of soon re-viewing their hero, with the captive English general to grace his triumph. The king's party were much dismayed in witnessing these vast preparations, and adjudged, with sad reluctance, the first victories to Bonaparte, reposing on the congregating forces of Europe, in case of the defeat of the English Army, to consummate the object of the treaty of the allies. Napoleon, in the confidence of speedy and complete success, flew to head his army of the north; and only a very few days had elapsed, when an hundred and one discharges of artillery awoke the Parisians at an early hour, announcing what all had either hoped, or dreaded, the total defeat of the allies, against whom the emperor had hurled his thunders.

The details of this signal victory were waited for with impatience. Every visage was marked with exultation, or despair; but everyone expected, from the loud and lengthened morning thunder, that the *Veni, vidi, vici*, had taken place. The bulletin appeared. It was modest, and reserved. It spoke indeed of victory, which the royalists interpreted into at least a drawn battle, but which the Bonapartists were assured was only a gentle preliminary hint that the extermination of the hostile armies would be next announced, as the combat was still raging. The news of the following day were awaited with seeming complacency by those last; who, hearing no sound of cannon, and seeing no bulletin, crowded to the hotel of the war department, where they learnt from official communications made by the minister, or the minister's secretaries, that the French had once more immortalised themselves in the plains of Fleurus; that the enemy had been overthrown on every point; that Blücher had flown back with his Prussians to Namur, and Wellington with his routed army to Brussels, in extreme confusion, and with incalculable loss. The official account stated, that the defeat of the Prussians was so complete, that there was no expectation of further news of them for some time, and with respect to the English:

> We shall see, in the course of a day or two, what we shall do with them—The emperor is there.

The emperor was there, to repeat the expression of the empty menace: but in what colours should be painted the rage, the despair, the confusion, the exultation, the excessive joy of the various parties, when, on the morning of the 20th June, after two days of painful surmise, and trembling expectation, it was whispered throughout Paris, "The emperor is here!" No one deigned to inquire what was the fate of the army. His presence in Paris was a bulletin too unequivocal of its entire defeat to need further confirmation. This act of cowardice had of late years been habitual to Bonaparte, and his arrival was always the signal of dire distress. A bulletin appeared in the afternoon, giving a long detail of the various combats that had taken place in this campaign of three or four days. But though the apprehensions of evil had been strongly raised, they attained not the detail of the disgrace and horror with which this official recital was filled.

> What! is such the result of all this dreadful preparation? Is it thus that our high-sounding hero fulfils his lofty promises? Is this the end of all his boastings when he flew to the frontier? His army, he says, was frightened. Is it thus that he attempts to mask his personal cowardice by a calumny on the victims of his madness and want of skill? His army has perished bravely in attacks to which his rashness has exposed them; and while his noble enemy was hazarding his person to ensure success, he stood aloof from danger to witness his defeat, and fled precipitately from the field to Paris to be the first herald of his own disgrace.

Such were the avowals and reproaches of the Bonapartean faction. The triumph of the citizens in general was decent and reserved; they feared the despair of the emperor's satellites. The tear of joy, the silent embrace, the ejaculatory thanksgiving to heaven, marked their demeanour. "Can it be true, and are we then delivered?" was repeated ten thousand times.

Bonaparte, on reviewing his hosts at Avesnes, after enumerating the Saxons, the Hanoverians, the Belgians, the Confederates of the Rhine, and other armies of the coalition said:

> Soldiers, they have lost their senses, blinded by a moment of prosperity. The oppression and humiliation of the French na-

tion is out of their power; if they enter France they will only find their graves; for every Frenchman who has courage feels that the moment is arrived either to conquer or perish.

This speech was addressed to them after reminding them of the fields of Marengo, of Friedland, of Austerlitz, and Wagram. The march began. The frontiers were passed in spite of the remonstrances of his generals; the retreating movements of the Prussians were described as signal victories. Joy brightened his crest. He was drunk with hope on reconnoitring the English Army. A council of war was held in the morning. He reluctantly seemed to yield to the opinions of all his generals, that it was prudent to suspend the attack. But before they rose from a repast to which he had invited them, the noise of the artillery told them what account he had made of their advice. In a moment of inspiration he had secretly given the orders, and his generals had only to repair to their respective posts.

General ——— said to me:

I stood by him, on a rising ground, and at a convenient distance. His astonishment at the resistance of the British Army was extreme. His agitation became violent. He took snuff by handfuls on the repulse of each charge. He exclaimed, 'These English are devils. They ought to have given in two hours since.' Ere the decisive blow was struck, he took me by the arm, 'Come, general, the affair is over—we have lost the day—let us be off.'

Bonaparte, who was not ill read in history, did not recollect a trait of the death of Scipio, the son-in-law of Pompey. When Scipio, after having been worsted in Africa, in support of Pompey, set sail for Spain, his fleet was surrounded by that of the enemy in his passage. The crew of his vessel surrendered. As soon as Scipio discovered it, he pierced himself with his sword. When Caesar's soldiers asked where was the general? the general answered, "He is where he ought to be," and then expired. This trait forms a curious contrast with the event of the memorable day of Waterloo. The grenadiers of the Imperial Guard, who fell with heroic courage on the field, had sworn to conquer or to die. English valour denied them victory, but could not prevent them from fulfilling the alternative of their oath—they died. The forest of Soignies is their grave. The soldiers are where they ought to be; but where is their general?

I shall not venture to give you a description of this combat, although I have heard it so often detailed both by the victors and the conquered. You will have read the various relations of this destructive day, which is recounted in fifty different ways by the actors; each describing things from the point of view in which he regarded the scene. A French general said:

"*Enfin*, I have served twenty years, I had never yet seen British troops. It is an army of heroes, the first army in Europe; I am yet in astonishment at what I witnessed."

"And their general," said I, "who was always classed by your emperor the second in the world?"

"What, Wellington? Bonaparte is a madman; he never equalled Wellington. Wellington is of no class, he is unique."

The general fought the battle over again in all its details, which I shall spare you, but which would form a volume. The subject of Wellington's glory was not new to me. The commanders who had served against him in Spain were unvaried in their opinion of his military talents. I have heard them often talk familiarly of their campaigns; had Bonaparte heard them also, he would have found that their opinion, and his own, respecting the military rank of Wellington, was not exactly the same. These officers, accustomed to such a waste of life on the *en avant* system, were, above all, struck by the avarice of blood which they observed in the English general.

This system of *en avant* was the great secret of Bonaparte's reputation. It is well known how much his mind is subject to superstition, and how firmly he believes in the influence of his star, and his predestined fate, or what he calls his *destin*. His star sometimes turned pale, and his *destin* assumed an aspect of mystery; but he trusted, and still believed. I was told by General ———, who was his first inspector of artillery, which answers to our master of ordnance, that the Battle of Eylau was at one moment lost. "General," said Bonaparte, "place your pieces so as to protect my retreat; it is all over; we are beaten.—You see how soon an empire is lost." The artillery was about to be placed, when four divisions of cavalry, that were not expected till the following day, suddenly made their appearance; the battle recommenced, and Bonaparte exclaimed, that his *destin* had the honours of the day.

In his successive flights from his army to Paris, Napoleon had always found some reason to allege in his excuse.[5] When he returned

---

5. The exclamation was repeated in Paris of an honest citizen of the Fauxbourg St. Antoine, who seeing the emperor pass on horseback, soon after the disaster of Moscow, said to his neighbour with great simplicity, "*Mais l'empereur se porte bien—il a bonne mine pas de tout l'air honteux.*"

from Russia he raised a smile, even in his servile senate, by attributing his disasters, not to the elements, or the enemy, the flames of Moscow, or the snows of the deserts, but threw the whole fault upon ideology, with which, he said, the senate had been occupied instead of furnishing him with fresh supplies. The loss of his army in Saxony he laid to the charge of some subaltern officer who had followed his orders in destroying a bridge which cut off the retreat of part of his troops. He now published in his bulletin, that the panic-terror of the army at Waterloo was the cause of the present defeat.

Bonaparte arrived in Paris at three in the morning, and assembled his counsellors. It was deemed by him necessary to try some masterstroke, something great and imperial, which should counterbalance the disgrace inflicted on him at Waterloo. After much deliberation, he thought that the evil impression made on the public mind, from the disaster occasioned by the pretended panic of the army, would be best neutralised by marching upon the assembly, and proclaiming himself Dictator. Lucien, his brother, was peremptory also in this opinion; but there were persons of the council whose minds were not bound up to such a terrible feat against the liberties of their country, and who declared their doubts whether even the instruments could readily be found, either among those called the Jacobins, or any part of the military. This discussion was not, however, so secret, but that some intimation of the brooding mischief reached a member of the House of Representatives, who had been too early skilled in revolutions, and had known Bonaparte too well, not to feel that no time was to be lost.

M. de la Fayette, gaining further assurance from two of the ministers, of the crime that was meditating, hurried to the house, which had assembled at an earlier hour than usual, as the news of Bonaparte's arrival had circulated through Paris. He found the president occupied in correcting some defects of grammar in the *procès-verbal* of the preceding day. He exclaimed:

Leave your *erratas*, there is other matter of discussion; hasten to open the sitting, and give me the parole.

Representatives, it is now twenty-five years since I raised my voice in this tribune of liberty; the country is in danger, and can be saved by you alone. The sinister reports, which have circulated these two days past, are unhappily confirmed. It is you whom it behoves to rally the whole country around the national standard, the standard of 1789, of liberty, equality, and public order; it is to you to whom it belongs to defend the independence and the honour of France against the pretensions of the enemy.

A veteran in the cause of liberty, a stranger to the spirit of faction, I am come to propose to you the previous measures which the crisis into which the nation is plunged demands; I am assured that all my colleagues will feel their necessity.

The first of these propositions was to declare that the independence of the country is threatened; the second, that the house shall declare itself permanent; that all attempts to dissolve it are high treason, and that any one who shall be guilty of this crime shall be immediately arraigned as a traitor to his country. The third proposition consisted of thanks to the army, and the national guard; the fourth was an invitation to the minister of the interior to convoke the staff officers of the national guard, and procure arms for every citizen who should be called to serve in it; the last was an invitation to the ministers to repair to the House, and answer all questions that should be made them.

No explanation was demanded by any member of the cause of these alarming propositions; it was sufficient that they were made by M. de la Fayette, and that Bonaparte was in Paris. The three first of these motions were immediately converted into laws. The national guard flocked round the assembly without waiting a law; but the ministers obeyed the summons of the chamber with less alacrity.

The discussion respecting the Dictatorship was yet carried on at the Elysée Palace, when intelligence was brought to Napoleon, that M. de la Fayette was then at the tribune, and haranguing the assembly. Bonaparte was trifling over his cup of coffee; "La Fayette at the tribune!" said he. The spoon dropt from his hand; the plot was discovered, and the discussion was adjourned.[6]

---

6. All intercourse between Bonaparte and M. de la Fayette had ceased for several years. M. de la Fayette was greatly indebted to Bonaparte for his intervention at the time of the treaty of Leoben, which rescued him from the dungeons of Olmutz. On his return to France, at the period of the 18th *Brumaire*, La Fayette, who had other ideas of glory than Bonaparte, believed that the latter meant to establish the liberties of his country. But, after several serious conversations with him, M. de la Fayette discovered his error, and refused to take any part in public affairs, though pressed by Bonaparte, and his friends, to accept the senatorial dignity. His restrictive vote against the consulship for life broke off all further communication between him and Bonaparte, and occasioned that noble letter to the first consul, which was found in the papers of Mr. Fox, and published in London, (continued next page),

It is very doubtful whether Bonaparte could have succeeded in his project of becoming Dictator, even if his attempt had not been baffled by the timely propositions of General la Fayette; but the lofty attitude which the assembly had now taken rendered all hopes of success fruitless. Recourse was therefore had to negotiation. The ministers, who had loitered in the council of the Elysée by the emperor's order, at length appeared on a second requisition, before the assembly, accompanied by Lucien Bonaparte, as imperial commissary, who required a committee of the whole house to communicate an imperial message. This message, which began by an elaborate recital of the misfortunes that had befallen the army, concluded with the information that the emperor had named a commission of three of his ministers to treat for peace with the allies.

The members, who were led to suppose, from the former part of this message, that Bonaparte's desire of being released from all further cares of government, would necessarily follow the avowal of his defeat, were astonished, in their turn, at this most lame and impotent conclusion. They expressed themselves in no measured terms upon the project of the emperor's treating for peace, when he himself was the only obstacle to its accomplishment. They said:

Give us some idea of your new policy. What are your plans, your combinations? Europe has declared war against Napoleon alone. Let us have no secrets. Shew us the depth of the abyss, we shall find means to fathom it; but how can the emperor pretend to save the country?

Lucien, who on the 18th *Brumaire* had extricated his brother from a *mauvais pas* with the Legislative Body, was now without success. His invocations to public generosity, to their late oaths of fidelity, his accusations of levity against the French nation, were urged in vain. The indignation of the assembly ran high—M. de la Fayette said:

We have followed your brother across the sands of Africa, the deserts of Russia; the bones of our countrymen, that whiten the plains in almost every quarter of Europe, bear witness to

several years since. On the return of Napoleon from the Isle of Elba, his brother Joseph solicited M. de la Fayette to accept the dignity of the peerage, and assured him that the emperor had placed him the first on the list. M. de la Fayette answered, that if he again appeared on the public scene it must be as representative of the people; and, having thus escaped being a peer, was named in his own department Member of the House of Representatives.

our patience and fidelity; it is our perseverance that we have to regret, and the blood of three millions of Frenchmen. Go, tell your brother that we will trust him no longer; we will ourselves undertake the salvation of our country.

Lucien and the ministers had nothing to reply to the gravity of these observations. They had themselves anticipated the sentiments of the assembly; and returned to conjure the emperor to send in his resignation. It was resolved, at the same time, to convene this night a great council, at the Tuileries, of all the ministers, of several counsellors of state, and of five members of each house of legislature. The president of this council was the Archi-Cchancelier Cambacerès. The emperor was not present. Various propositions were made respecting the modes of defence, and of raising supplies. The principal object of the meeting seemed to be evaded, or forgotten, when M. de la Fayette declared, that in adopting all that had been proposed for the defence of the country, the first object, that of the abdication, had not yet been mentioned; he then moved that the council, headed by the president, should present itself to the emperor, and make the demand.

This motion did not succeed. The council broke up at three in the morning, and the ministers, with the counsellors of state, and some deputies, repaired to the palace of the Elysée. The ministers were pressing for the abdication, and particularly the Duke d'Otrante, M. Constant, and two of the representatives. Napoleon persisted in his refusal till he learnt, by one of his counsellors, that if the abdication was not sent to the chamber within an hour, M. de la Fayette was determined to move for his expulsion. The respite of an hour was given for reflection, and the assembly adjourned for an hour; at the end of that time it resumed its sitting, and received the formal abdication of the imperial throne.

It was now that Bonaparte began to feel that the disgrace inflicted on him at Waterloo was about to receive its consummation at Paris, since the only expiation of his unskilfulness as general was the resignation of his crown as emperor. He was at length convinced that he could only prevent his expulsion by voluntary abdication. This seeming act of virtue was sent to each of the chambers, as a sacrifice he made to the peace of France, and the hatred of Europe, with the condition that the legislative bodies proclaimed his son. Napoleon the Second, Emperor of the French.

The assembly, without attending to the article respecting the young Napoleon, accepted solemnly, in the name of the French people, the abdication of Napoleon Bonaparte, and named a deputation, composed of the president, the vice president, and the secretaries, to offer him the thanks of the chamber. It was an interesting spectacle, said one of the deputation to me, to behold those nine representatives of the people, invested only with the force of public opinion, and the decree of the assembly, entering the palace of this man, against whom a million of soldiers were in arms, who had given orders to all the sovereigns of the continent, who still commanded the French armies, the guard which surrounded him, and a numerous party in the Fauxbourgs, to announce to him that he was no longer emperor, and that the nation resumed the government.

He received the deputation, surrounded by all the great officers of his household, and those of his guard, with all the pomp suitable to the imperial dignity of which he was about to be deprived. His figure and deportment were calm; he said that a great disaster had happened, but that the territory was yet untouched; he spoke of the sacrifice which he made, at the desire of the chamber, to public circumstances, and to his tenderness for his son. The president observed to him, in a respectful tone, that the assembly, whose decree he had just read, had not deliberated on that part of his message, but that he would render an account count of His Majesty's observations.

"I thought so," said Bonaparte aside, to his brother, "I did not suppose they could do it;" but resuming, he answered, "Tell the Assembly that I recommend to it my son." The deputation withdrew, still observing the most respectful ceremonies.

What a crowd of reflexions present themselves on this memorable interview between Bonaparte, La Fayette, and Lanjuinais! The deputation, on their return to the assembly, demanded that the liberty and life of Napoleon should be put under the protection of the French nation. It was generally believed that he would depart immediately for the United States. It is certain that, had he lost no time, he might at this moment have escaped on board a small neutral vessel, in which an hiding-place was prepared. But he must have fled with only one servant. He hesitated, and loitered till it was too late, and, happily for the repose of mankind, his destiny led him to the *Bellerophon*.

Bonaparte had passed through the scene with the deputation of the Legislative Body, with dignity; and would have left an impression of respect, had it not been known that he was still acting a part. He had resigned the place of emperor, but that of dictator still occupied his mind. He had, on his arrival, interrogated on this subject a distinguished person, who was one of his last conquests, as he deemed it, from the popular party. "Can I not march upon the two chambers, and proclaim myself dictator? The deputies will do nothing, and there is no time to be lost."

"Your Majesty may physically execute, at this moment, what you intimate," replied his counsellor, "but be assured your power will not last three days;" alleging reasons for his opinion which Napoleon found unanswerable. But for some days after his resignation, the idea of the dictatorship and of the opinions he had heard from his counsellor, seemed still to haunt his mind; and when the cries of the Fédérés, of "*Vive Napoleon!*" from without the palace, reached his ear, he was heard repeating to himself, "It would be but for three days!"

The condition of the direct nomination of Napoleon's son to the succession was eluded as dexterously as possible by the deputies; the house passing to the order of the day, as a son naturally succeeded to his father; but stating at the same time by the reporter, that the safety of twenty millions could not be put in competition with the fortune of a child. The assembly thought it imprudent to come to a more open declaration. Bonaparte, though clothed with no legal authority, was still at his palace in the Champs Elysees, surrounded by soldiers, mingled with his old allies the mob, who saluted him with their licentious cries of "*Vive l'Empereur!* give us arms, we are ready to support our emperor." These effusions of popular sympathy operated on the sensibility of the fallen hero. The ex-emperor testified his gratitude, by humble greetings, and a certain number of arms were distributed to the populace. The assembly meanwhile convoked the chiefs of the legions of the national guard, and these citizen-soldiers formed a formidable and numerous *phalanx* around them.

The debates of the upper house, called the Chamber of Peers, were not carried on with the same order, and decent observance. An opposition arose from a quarter least expected. The man who was already consigned to infamy for his treason against the king, Marshal Ney, and who had commanded the right wing of the army at Waterloo, rose in his place, and gave what is called the lie direct to the whole of Carnot's favourable report respecting the state of the army. The ordinary gravity of this house was also interrupted by one of Napoleon's generals, La Bedoyère, the first officer who had joined him on his landing, and had delivered up Grenoble. Some hesitation in the house had been discerned by him, respecting the condition exacted in Napoleon's act of abdication, that of the nomination of young Napoleon as emperor. This officer said:

"If, you don't acquiesce, the emperor will draw his sword, and he will yet be unsparing of blood. The nation is unworthy of his affection towards it."

The speech of this raving *Seid* was answered calmly by Massena, "You are much too young, M. le Général."

M. Lameth added, "that M. La Bedoyère had forgotten he was no longer in the guard-house." Nothing farther was decided respecting the succession of Napoleon the Second.

It being impossible to carry on business without an executive government, and not unlikely that Napoleon might repent of his abdication, five persons were named to take the supreme command. These were M. Fouché, Duke d'Otrante, minister of the police; M. Carnot, the minister for home affairs; M. de Caulincourt, the minister of the foreign department; the General Grenier; and M. Quinette, members of the upper house. The first operation of this commission was the nomination of five persons to go and demand peace from the allies. No great hopes were entertained of the success of their mission, of the propriety of which, however, no one doubted; since the allies had declared that it was not against France that they had made war, but against Bonaparte only, who was no longer the chief of the empire.

The legislative assemblies were not yet completely aroused from their stupor, when fear, or prudence had led them to admit, or pass over Napoleon's nomination of his son for his successor, as the condition of his abdication. They were yet, the great majority at least, much exhilarated with the incident of the imperial resignation; although they still doubted the sincerity of this descent, as they knew how well skilled he was in trick and stratagem. When the news of the death of Commodus was brought to the Roman senate, those Conscript Fathers doubted the truth of the event; but when assured that the tyrant really existed no longer, they were tumultuous in the expressions of their indignation against him; devoting his name to everlasting infamy, and ordering the exposure of his remains on the theatre of the gladiators.

Commodus was dead, and could not retaliate; but Bonaparte was still alive, and at his well guarded palace in Paris. The prudent apprehensions of the degraded Roman senate may perhaps form an apology for the French senate, whose tyrant had not yet paid the forfeit of life; and though he had witnessed the sacrifice of his imperial guard, there yet remained a number sufficient of these minions of despotism, added to the stupid fanaticism of some corps of regular troops, and the Paris mob, to make him formidable, when the caprice of resuming his power should seize him. There were many who longed to treat his memory with as little ceremony as those Romans did their fallen tyrants; but they prudently pondered on the maxim of Marius, appropriated by Barrère, "*Qu'il n'y a que les morts qui ne reviennent pas;*" and felt that it was not impossible that Bonaparte might again start up as emperor.

LETTER 11

July, 1815.

The Parisians had been amused during the two last months in fortifying the heights round Paris. The national guard had been put in requisition for that purpose, each battalion in its turn to lend their aid to this work of fortification. The Bonapartists had not forgotten the ardour with which the Parisians of all ages, and even of each sex, had lent their aid to prepare the Champs de Mars, for the first great federation, and they hoped to call forth the same enthusiasm. But all that now passed was a miserable mockery indeed, of the first bright moments of the revolution. France was no longer a nation rousing itself like "*the strong man from sleep, and shaking his invincible locks!*" All the noble promises of liberty had proved faithless, all its altars had been profaned.

Many of the national guard refused to share the labours of the spade, and those who went to the barriers, after working a few hours, and partaking together of a convivial repast, usually returned home with their backs strained by this new exercise.

The services, however, of the national guard, claim the eternal gratitude of their fellow-citizens. They have stood in the breach, and rescued us alike from military and popular oppression; they have nobly earned the civic wreath; they have been the tutelar guardians of our hearths; their patriot virtues have acquired the respect even of strangers; conquering armies have chosen them for their auxiliaries in the maintenance of public tranquillity and order; and their bleeding country, in the hour of danger, has not leaned in vain upon their shield.

The allied armies now drew near the city. Their approach had been concealed as long as possible; we had heard of plenipotentiaries, suspension of arms, the defection of Austria from the other coalised pow-

74

ers, the arrival of a considerable part of the Grand Army in good order. But the reign of subterfuge and deception was at an end. The answer to all the eloquent declamations of the Bonapartists was the arrival of crowds of flying peasantry seeking refuge within the walls of the capital. The experience of the foregoing year had taught us what was meant by these sad rustic processions, which in the same manner had preceded the memorable day of battle—disastrous images of a country in distress,—the long line of carts which followed one another in slow succession, each filled with the household wealth of the owner, who himself helped to drag on his wearied horse. On these rustic vehicles were placed not what Belvidera calls "*the massy domestic ornaments*," but old family utensils, worn mattresses, and chairs, and tables in decay, and a little store of hay and corn, provision for the horse, and a cow which followed tied behind the cart.

The fugitives were fewer in number than on the same occasion last year. The country-people had learnt that the invading army was that of the English, and they had heard that the English troops are an exception to the general practice of plunder and devastation; that they never ill-treated the inhabitants; that they paid liberally for what they wanted, and caressed the little children. The excellent reputation they had acquired last year in the South had flown over France to the North; and it was well known that wherever the English passed, the unarmed inhabitant had nothing to fear. A friend of mine wrote to me from the South:

Lord Wellington will soon pass near our *château*, but we shall remain in perfect security—all is safe where they appear.

Many of the peasants who had ventured to remain in their dwellings had suffered cruelly from the merciless rapine of the French, and were perhaps disposed to exclaim, "Save me from my friends." They were filled with astonishment when they beheld an armed host, four abreast, pause when about to enter the field of wheat, in crossing the country, and changing their order proceed in Indian files, one by one, along the narrow beaten path, careful to do no injury by treading on the corn, and avoid "bruising the flowerets of the valley with hostile paces."

In a little village called Vertu, two leagues from Paris, the English troops, on their arrival, told the inhabitants they must dislodge immediately: but, to the great surprise of the peasants, the soldiers set themselves to work, and helped them to remove their little furniture, carefully avoiding to break or injure any thing by precipitation. "*Comme ils sont bons! comme ils sont bons!*" was repeated a thousand times by these poor people on their entering Paris. What a proud tribute of praise for a conquering general is contained in those simple words issuing from the lips of the vanquished! What an additional lustre does virtue shed over those high achievements which fill so bright a page in the records of military renown, and which have had so signal an influence on the destinies of the world!

The name of Wellington was never pronounced without veneration by his enemies, or the pride of patriotic exultation by his friends; he, who has softened the terror of his arms with such a benignant ray of moral glory, and has taught his victorious bands, amidst the ardour of conquest, the avarice of blood. Others may have deserved the wreaths of courage, but who has ever blended them, like him, with the pure and white palms of philanthropy? Others may claim the praise of able generals, but to Wellington will be ascribed the denomination of the Great Captain. He has exalted valour by an inseparable and sublime connection with mercy; and to the history of his exploits may be applied, what the celebrated Mrs. Montagu observed of the writings of the great English moralist, that "*an angel might give the imprimatur.*"

What a singular picture did that part of the Boulevard present, where the fugitives arrived! The passage of the Porte St. Martin was almost entirely obstructed by the crowd of Parisians, mingled with the peasantry, and their *cortège* of wearied animals—on one side of the *boulevard* the people were struggling for admission to the celebrated new piece of the "*Pie Voleuse*,"—the Thieving Magpie; on the other, a little black horse dragged along the cart, or ambulant shop, which ever since the departure of Louis XVIII. has been established on the boulevard for the sale of M. Carnot's famous pamphlet on Regicide; once sold at six *francs*, and now offered to the public at the moderate and reduced price of twelve *sous* a copy.

Farther on, a portion of the remains of the imperial guard were marching along, "*pride in their port, defiance in their eye*," thundering out "*Vive l'Empereur!*" and one of them striking with his sabre a poor old man, who had the imprudence to articulate, in a feeble voice, "*Mes amis, criez Vive le Roi!*" Five or six persons on this day fell the victims of this forbidden exclamation by the hands of those *Praetorian* bands. The small number of them that survived the battle of Waterloo had returned with rage in their bosoms at their defeat, and despair at the abdication of their chief. They well knew that all they had done, and suffered, found no answering voice of sympathy from the people of Paris, except amongst the lowest multitude. In general, the mass of the Parisians, rankled by calamity, felt far more horror for the tyrant, than pity for his voluntary victims; and although no people have more sensibility than the French to the splendour of military achievements, yet now, in the bitterness of their hearts for the evils they had undergone, and those with which they were menaced, they might well be permitted to observe of the heroical courage of the imperial guard, "Curse on their virtues, they've undone their country!"

Bonaparte, after several disagreeable altercations with some of his late ministers, now become his masters, withdrew from Paris to Malmaison. His continuance at Paris had begun to excite considerable alarm. *"The snake was scotched, not killed."* Old Napoleon was yet alive for his son. These apprehensions had been increased by the daily entrance of corps of regular troops into the capital, with the accustomed cries of *"Vive l'Empereur;"* and of whose concurrence Bonaparte was assured whenever he might think it expedient to exert his imperial energies. Rumours of menacing tendency were spread abroad; the means of evil were still in Napoleon's power, and he would not neglect the occasion. The provisionary government,, who were too highly interested in his movements not to watch them with an attentive eye, invited him, in terms that could not be misunderstood, to withdraw from Paris.

During a few days previous to his departure, he appeared meditative, and much employed; it was however on his own personal affairs. His attention was turned to the new world whither he was going. You may perhaps suppose that the examples of those Roman heroes who could not outlive their honourable defeat on the plain of Philippi, might have occurred to his remembrance; or he of Pontus, who, though out of the reach of Pompey, sought no further refuge than the Cimerian Bosphorus, by the double instrument of poison and the sword. You may imagine that he was reflecting on the friendly offers of his faithful Mameluke, who, on his abdication the preceding year at Fontainebleau, stood before him with his newly-sharpened scimitar, saying that he waited his orders to perform the last duty. The examples of Cato of Utica, of Hannibal, and of so many other illustrious personages, you may believe glided through his mind. No, Bonaparte's thoughts were remote from these heathenish deeds of greatness; his meditations were of a more sober and familiar nature.

The preparations with which he was busied at this eventful moment, "*big with his fate,*" were those of Perkal, and perfumery; and his discourse was of the cut, size, and quality of various kinds of shirts, and the quantity of *pomatums* and perfumes which he judged necessary for his expedition. The inventory of those objects which he has left behind him, is not the least curious fragment found among the collection of his state-papers. It appears that no detail was omitted or neglected for the voyage he was preparing to make towards the new world, in the well-stored cabin of a light frigate; and as to his return to our hemisphere, he left that affair at present to his *destin*. He had in the meantime written to the government from his retreat at Malmaison, and solicited to be named *generalissimo* of the army, to defend Paris, and save the country. But as the government did not think proper to confide either the defence of Paris, or the salvation of the country to his exertions, his demand was rejected.

Relieved from the task of governing the world, Bonaparte cheered the monotony of his retreat by conversations not only with the military, but with some men of letters and artists, who visited him at Malmaison, and the chief topic of his discourse with those persons was the errors and abuses of his own government; but in discussing the late events, he always spoke in the third person, and as if he himself had no immediate concern in those operations, said he:

> The emperor appears to have acted, in this instance, from such and such motives; and in that, to obtain such results, but he did wrong in both instances. The emperor trusted to information that was unfounded. He was too precipitate, or too tardy; he made mistakes which he might easily have avoided, and calculated upon mistakes of his adversaries, which they did not commit.

Bonaparte was in the vein of being communicative; and happening to overhear a speedy answer given by a professional man to a question of an importunate neighbour, respecting the state of his wife, Bonaparte abandoned his *critique* on the emperor's errors, and began an harangue of three quarters of an hour, and without discontinuing, on the obstetrical art. Then resuming the tone of the emperor, he declaimed against the present practice; declaring that it was his intention to have proposed various ameliorations in the schools, some of which he mentioned. Thus, in imitation of a famous warrior of antiquity, (Mithridates), almost as great a destroyer of the human race as himself, and who had written a treatise on the secret of diseases, or the art of healing, Bonaparte seemed to have had the project of writing on this professional subject. He might, perhaps, have been no less dangerous to mankind in its embryo state, as a surgeon, than he had been to adults, as a general.

The distance which the ex-emperor had placed between himself and the Parisians, was not deemed sufficient. The government invited him again to quit his Tusculum, and repair to his destination at Rochefort, where the frigates awaited him. Napoleon's departure from Malmaison was an assurance to the higher classes of their personal safety, and who had dreaded nothing more than the defence of Paris by him and his army. Their defeat beyond the walls of Paris was too probable, and would have drawn on the destruction of the city, which would have been inevitably pillaged by its defenders, if it were spared by the allies. The allegiance of the Parisians was transferred to the Duke of Wellington, as their only protector. The entrance of the English Army was anxiously looked for, and it was a subject of murmurs, that the commander of Paris delayed their deliverance.

The legislature, in the meantime, was earnestly occupied in fabricating a new constitution, which was to be offered to the acceptance of whoever should take the sovereign authority, arid this was the standing business, or order of the day. Commissaries were occasionally dispatched from the Chamber to exchange compliments with the troops without the walls, or, in the old civic language, to fraternize the deputies proclaiming Napoleon the Second, while the troops adhered to Napoleon the First, and cried long live that emperor, with whom only they were acquainted. A few of the imperial guards, who had a better comprehension of the affair, understanding that their old emperor no longer commanded them, having abdicated, deemed it wiser to withdraw, than fight for they knew not whom. Being reprimanded by their colonel, on the *boulevards* in Paris, for their desertion of their post, they answered sternly, that they had too much honour to desert; "*mais nous avons abdiqué.*"

The French Army around Paris, notwithstanding the publicity of the imperial abdication, appeared to doubt of its truth. They declared that it was some trick of state, and that they knew their emperor too well to believe he would resign. This reminds me of the German who, when a report was spread through Germany, several years since, that Bonaparte was dead, exclaimed, "*Bonaparte mort! Vous le connaissez fort peu—il s'en gardera bien.*"

Napoleon had dispatched a farewell letter to the French Army under the walls of Paris, dated from Malmaison, the 25th June, 1815. This letter was addressed to the heroes of the army, and no doubt the lowest drummer fancied he saw his own name on the direction.

> Soldiers, in yielding to the necessity which separates me from the brave French Army, I am confident that by its eminent services, it will merit that praise from its country, which is not refused even by its enemies. Soldiers, I shall follow your steps, though absent. I know every corps, and not one of them will gain any signal advantage without my having kept an account of the bravery it shall have shewn. We have both been calumniated, you, and myself. Soldiers, a few more efforts, and the coalition is dissolved. Napoleon will be grateful for the strokes you are about to inflict. Save the honour and the independence of the French. Be, to the last, the men I have known you for twenty years, and you will be invincible.

This letter of *adieu* was distributed to the army. It intimated absence, but the absent might return, of which himself was the proof. That he would return, they believed firmly, and had his death been announced, they would probably have expected his resurrection. Even the belief of his absence was by no means general; it was imagined, that he was lurking in some shape or other in their ranks, and that he would stand up in his own, whenever the great day of general contest should take place.

The first attack made by the allied armies was to the north of Paris, and was confined to skirmishes and distant cannonade. At three in the morning, on the 30th June, I was awakened by the first roar of cannon, not as it is usually heard in popular cities, the sign of victory, the symbol of public festivity, but the harbinger of woe, the messenger of death. The first cannon was fired from the heights of Belleville, which nearly front my window. I arose immediately. What contrasts the scene presented, and what dissonant sounds struck my ear! The sky was tinged with the first soft colours of the morning, and the hills and gardens covered with the freshest verdure, except where the Butte of Chaumont on the right, and the heights of Montmartre on the left, presented their formidable artillery, which was at that moment pouring forth its horrible contents; while, at intervals of silence, the note of earliest birds floated along the air, and seemed to reproach mankind for this disturbance of nature. Strongly impressed with the events of the last year, I was too much alarmed at the probable events of the present.

On the 30th March, 1814, I had been awakened also, at the first dawn of day, by the roar of cannon placed on the very same theatre, that of the hills, which overlook my windows. The cannonade on that day was long, loud, and tremendous. The volleys of artillery were almost incessant during twelve hours. Shells had torn up the gardens around us, and our only refuge was to retire behind the walls of the house, which we hoped were too thick for cannon balls to penetrate. That day had indeed been awful till, at six in the evening, the capitulation being announced, the tumult of battle gave place to the sounds of music; and some of the soldiers of the French army, and those of the allies, joined the nymphs of the Fauxbourg in the sprightly dance, forgetful, alas! of their fallen comrades.

The attack on the 30th June, 1815, was far less formidable. It was chiefly confined to musketry, and slackened very sensibly at six in the morning. Notwithstanding the fortifications on the heights, the city might have been entered on this side, but the slaughter must have been excessive; and the Duke of Wellington, who knew well the ground around Paris, made himself master of the best positions; and no longer attempting an entrance on the north, the allied army drew off by the river, towards Neuilly and St. Germain.

The musketry, which had continued in the plain of St. Denis, ceased altogether at about three in the afternoon. I then went on the *boulevards*; all the gay shops that enliven that brilliant walk were closely shut up, and what sinister presages might be read in every visage of the crowd! On examining the hostile passions pourtrayed in every countenance, it seemed as if the assembled multitudes waited only the signal for civil war. We appeared to be treading on a mine ready to receive the spark of explosion. The swarms of the Fauxbourgs St. Antoine and St. Marceau were let loose. They had taken no part in public events, since their time of active citizenship in the days of terror. But their dormant patriotism was now awakened, bribed or whipped up, and they issued from their retreats with the hope of being active in some extraordinary scene.

Many "*a smith was there, swallowing a taylor's news.*" Some of the figures in the group were Les Forts de la Halle,—corn and coal-porters. They had formed a part of the federative deputation of the two *fauxbourgs* to the emperor, of late styled "*l'Empereur de la Canaille;*" and offered their military services. The emperor, on account of their enormous round white and black hats, had pleasantly named them *Ses mousquetaires noirs et blancs*. These groups were composed of women, as

81

well as men, for nothing ever passes in Paris, great or minute, without the interference of women; and some might have claimed the palm from the other sex, in clamour and vociferation.

The French commander-in-chief, who was the minister of war, had taken his headquarters at La Villette, just without the walls of Paris. From thence, as the military business of the preceding day was of no great importance, a correspondence was established by the minister and his staff, with the Chamber of Deputies, and by himself with the Duke of Wellington.

The minister said:

Representatives of the people, we are in presence of the enemy. We swear before you, and the whole world, that we will defend to our latest breath the cause of our independence, and the honour of the nation. They wish to force the Bourbons upon us. The Bourbons give no pledge to the nation, &c.

This address was signed by Davoust, and fourteen generals. The letter to the Duke of Wellington contained a formal demand of a cessation of hostilities, since the object of the war, Napoleon's abdication, was accomplished. The Duke of Wellington's object was not yet accomplished, which was that of the possession of Paris, with the least effusion of blood possible. He continued therefore to invest the city, by establishing posts at the distance of ten or twelve miles, at Versailles, St. Germain's, to the west of Paris, taking successive possession of the heights, to the hills of Meudon, which overlook the town. These manoeuvres were effectuated with more or less interruption by the French, during the three days that followed that of the first attack in the plain of St. Denis.

While these formidable armies were in contest without the walls, for the possession of Paris, various were the alarms and terrors which agitated its inhabitants. At length, however, the report was generally circulated, that the allies were about to turn the siege into a blockade; that we had nothing to fear from pillage; and that we should only be starved. The arrival, however, of the accustomed provisions the next day, through the midst of the enemy's camp, led the Parisians to apply to Wellington, the well known trait of Henry the Fourth, when he besieged Paris.

On the 1st July the scene on the *boulevard* was quite changed since that of yesterday. The Parisians expected that the enemy would have entered on the first attack, and they were tired of the delay. They had heard the cannon at intervals during twenty-four hours; yesterday this was a novelty; but today they felt as if accustomed to be besieged, and returned to their usual avocations and pleasures. Yesterday the theatres were shut, which was indeed a striking signal of distress in Paris; today, though the great theatres were closed, the *"Thievish Magpie"* resumed his triumph at the theatre of the Porte St. Martin; and that of La Gaieté prepared for the public amusement the bombardment of Algiers, a melodrame fitted to fill up the interval of the great melodrame of national events. The barriers of Paris were prudently shut, and the field of battle without the walls was occupied only by military. Had not the Parisian women been refused egress, curiosity might perhaps have got the better of fear; they would have risked a wound, in the hope that it would not disfigure their faces; and the plains of St. Denis might have been strewed, not only with wrecks of cabriolets, and pleasure-carts, but with hats, caps, and other articles of millinery baggage.

In the evening the Italian Boulevard was crowded, as usual, with the gay tribes, who, seated on double rows of chairs, with an interval for the walkers, pass the latter part of their summer evenings, inhaling the dust in good company. This evening, the walk, as usual, had its itinerant band of music, its ices in the adjoining *cafés*, and all its accustomed attractions.

It may be observed, that the Italian Boulevard, so long the haunt of the fashionable world of Paris, has undergone various changes of name during the course of the Revolution. In the first years of that event, this *boulevard* was denominated, or was rather stigmatized, by the appellation of Coblentz, on account of its being frequented by that class of society of which a great part had emigrated to that place. On the departure of Louis the Eighteenth, and the return of Bonaparte, Coblentz was subdivided into the Boulevard de Gand, (Ghent,) and the Boulevard de l'île d'Elbe. The former is, at the moment I am writing, brilliant, with a thousand wreaths of fresh-blown lilies twined round every hat, while the latter, that of Elba, is abandoned to the faction of the scarlet pink and the violet. But to return to the evening of the first of July.—The amusements of the *boulevard* were occasionally varied by the march of troops, the beating to arms, the swift pace of couriers, the sound of cannon at intervals; and sometimes all gaiety was suspended by the sad spectacle of the wounded victims of those skirmishes, writhing in agony and covered with blood.

I heard one young officer, who was borne along on planks by four of his men, and who was mortally wounded, exclaim as he passed,

"Achevez-moi, mes amis, achevez-moi—vous voyez que je meurs—vive la patrie!" "Finish me, my friends, put an end to my sufferings; yes, I see I must die; heaven preserve my country!" It may be supposed that in the heat of battle, such an affecting appeal, and such a noble exclamation might pass unnoticed; but here, at home, amidst his countrymen, and even women, to find no sympathy, not *"as much pity as would fill the eye of a wren;"* no tender tear from any female spectator—no interest but that of simple curiosity. Oh! how the spirit of party shuts up every avenue to the heart; how it blunts every better feeling, how it renders us cruel, and almost wicked!

Though no one was permitted to go out of Paris, all were suffered to enter; and we had frequent news of what was passing without. I met a sprightly young captain, who told me that he had yesterday been prisoner to the English, and then began the praises of our countrymen.

> We thrashed the Prussians the day before, and we had fixed a party of about a dozen to breakfast together yesterday. We saw presently that we were pursued by a superior number of English officers. We rode hard, having more appetite for breakfast than fighting. I rose in one stirrup to look around at them, they were still in pursuit. My saddle turned round, and I fell to the ground. *Me voilà dans une belle position!* They came up, and surrounded me; I thought myself a dead man, for we had not spared the Prussians the preceding day. What was my surprise when I saw they were occupied in re-saddling my horse! 'Come, get up, sir, if you are not hurt; we shall take no advantage of the negligence of your groom.'

The British and Prussian forces had now drawn nearer Paris, and on Monday, the 3rd July, the armies were in presence in the plain of Grenelle, to the south-west of the city. The French Army was in possession of the plain, directly under the walls; the allies were ranged on the heights of the villages of Issy, Venvres, and Meudon. The morning passed in preparations and manoeuvres for battle. Many persons went in their carriages to the bridge of Jena, which is the passage to the field. As the carriages arrived near the bridge, they were immediately put in requisition; the persons within were desired to alight, and were told that the battle was about to begin, and that their carriages were borrowed to transport the wounded. In vain did some ladies remonstrate against this military mandate; in vain they appealed to the commander of the guard. They were told with more truth than gallantry, that they were well able to walk; and it was hinted to them, that if they did not withdraw, he might be obliged to put them also in requisition to attend the wounded.

The houses of Chailliot within the city walls overlook the whole of this plain, and the surrounding hills. We were informed that the signal of battle was to be given at four in the afternoon. This was indeed an awful moment, the horror of which was heightened by the circumstance that the great magazine of powder is placed on the plain of Grenelle; and that not only the combatants on either side might become the victims of an explosion, but the city itself might be covered with ruins. Is there no pitying angel hovering on celestial wing to avert this horrible crash? If the demon of war must rage along those hostile ranks, spare, oh spare this devoted city! Paris belongs not to the French alone; all Europe is interested in its preservation; in its science, its literature, its arts; all that it contains of the accumulated riches of the civilized world. The destruction of those treasures, the legacy of genius to future ages, would be less a national loss, than a calamity to be deplored by mankind, a crime to be arraigned by posterity!

Far removed indeed from such barbarous hostility was the mind of that general who had now led on his triumphant army from the immortal field of Waterloo, to the gates of Paris. His first care was to prevent superfluous misery; to pour no useless drop into the cup of bitterness. He wished to avoid the horrors of a battle; his volume of glory was too amply filled to want one additional page of splendour. He had already snatched kingdoms from the tyrant's grasp; he had lately achieved a more difficult task; he had met the vaunting conqueror of Europe at the head of the most formidable armies; he had laid his renowned legions in the dust; he had torn the imperial crown from his brow, and driven him from his usurped empire, the capital of which he was about to enter. The Duke of Wellington invited the French generals to a conference; he leads them through his ranks; he displays his positions, his plans, his resources; he grants them the necessary time for deliberation: the sword is returned to its scabbard, and Paris is spared! An honourable capitulation was granted, and the conqueror received the most glorious recompense of his forbearance, that of the gratitude of the vanquished.

LETTER 12

July, 1815.
Agreeably to the terms of the capitulation, signed on the 3rd July,

the French Army began, on the following day, its inarch beyond the Loire, and the allied armies took possession of the posts and villages nearest the walls of Paris, such as St. Denis, St. Ouen, Clichy, Neuilly, &c. On the second day of the surrender, Montmartre, now become a citadel, was put into their power, and on the day following the barriers, or gates of Paris.

Thus, in the short space of fifteen months, was the capital of France twice besieged, and twice compelled to open its gates and receive the law of the conqueror—Paris, the triumphant city;—Paris, which the revolutionary orator had surnamed the *Chef lieu du globe!*—How are the mighty fallen!—"Tell it not in Gath, publish it not in Askalon!"—Where are now the invincible armies of France, so long accustomed to go forth, led on by Glory? Where are those irresistible legions that never fought but to conquer? What is become of those innumerable bands of heroic youths she had called into the field, and whose brows were bound with all the trophies of intrepid valour? Where are the heroes of Marengo, of Austerlitz, of Jena, of Wagram? Alas! they have been swept away "in the pride of their days" by their merciless leader! Their mothers are childless, and their wives are widows! They have perished on the icy banks of the Borysthenes, or fell buried under the snows of the desert.

In vain, as they hastened from the conflagrated capital of the northern world, the wounded soldier, stretched on the earth, implored the retreating hosts, as they passed by, to aid him in his distress, to stretch out an hand to raise him up!—In vain, with uplifted eyes, did he remind them of the fraternal ties of comrade, so sacred to the soldier's bosom! The frank and open heart was now steeled by its own misery, absorbed by its own dangers, hardened into selfishness by intolerable sufferings, rendered inexorable by its own desperation. The appeal of the expiring soldier for mercy was heard by his comrade, and he passed sullenly on. No one paused to listen to the last groan of those unhappy youths, of whom many, torn for the first time from home, repeated in dying, the dearest, tenderest of names—the name of mother!

The tranquillity of the city was not disturbed by any triumphal entry, as on the last year. The national guard, who kept the barriers, were relieved by foreign troops, and observed the same order and good humour, as if these soldiers had been their comrades. I saw about a thousand people assembled at the barriers of the Champs Elysees to witness the ceremony; which they did with a careless air, and seemed disposed to receive the allies, as Catherine of Medicis did the head of

Admiral Coligny,

Sans crainte, sans plaisir, maîtresse de ses sens,
Et comme accoutumée à de pareils présens.

The only disappointment they seemed to feel was that of having no grand spectacle, for "is this all" was everywhere repeated, when the guard was exchanged. The martial pomp of last year had furnished a sight memorable indeed. A procession opened by emperors, and kings, with crowds of finely accoutred generals, and closed by two hundred thousand men, parading along the *boulevards*. It must also be observed, that one of the most striking circumstances in the march of this conquering army through the streets of the capital, was the modest demeanour of those warlike hosts. They displayed no other sign of victory than a branch of laurel which decorated their hats, and even this slight badge of success was softened by a white scarf tied round the arm of every soldier, as the proffered pledge of amity and peace.

The pretended barbarians of the north seemed to have learnt from the generous monarchs who led them on, a sentiment which belongs to the highest state of civilization and refinement, that of fearing, even by a look, to insult the feelings of the vanquished. You will easily believe that the exclamation above-mentioned, "is this all," and the wish for a grand spectacle, was confined to what is called the "people." Every enlightened Frenchman, every liberal mind, every true lover of his country, wept tears of blood at its cruel, its reiterated humiliation. They had not been guilty of the crime of having conquered Europe, but they were doomed to share the punishment, and to deplore its intolerable disgrace—disgrace felt at every moment, and seen in every object.

But if the surrender of Paris wounded the feelings of national pride, no real patriot had wished to see the city defended. A vain and hopeless defence had been deprecated by all, except by the enraged Fédérés of the Fauxbourgs, who sought for a share in spoil and pillage; and, I must add also, by a few strangers who had nothing to risk, or to lose. One of these, a celebrated historian, was descanting, in a society of the great and the opulent, upon the duty of resistance, and the ignominy of surrender; when a friend of mine observed, "*on voit que Monsieur n'a rien à Paris que son écritoire.*"—"It appears that this gentleman has nothing at Paris but his ink-horn." We have, indeed, too often had occasion to observe, that strangers seem to arrive in France, as they would go to a *melodrame*, prepared for extraordinary events, and where the deeper the tragedy the better they are entertained.

It is difficult to imagine any thing more calculated to irritate those who suffer, than to observe curiosity substituted for sympathy by those around them, unless it be to hear the author of these calamities extolled in the presence of his victims. Nothing surprised the French more, during the reign of Napoleon, than to hear the declamations of some English visitors in his favour. Those strangers could scarcely guess what an effect such panegyric produced on a Parisian circle, necessarily composed, in part at least, of persons who had suffered from imperial tyranny. It required the whole stock of French courtesy to suppress, on these occasions, the feelings of resentment, and which were the more difficult to stifle from the novelty of the provocation. It must be observed that for some years past no person in France ever praised the emperor, except in speeches to the throne. No minister, senator, or counsellor of state, would have ventured to outrage the feelings of society by saying one word in his favour in a private *salon*. These personages talked of Napoleon, with quite as little ceremony as others, among their friends; in mixed company they were silent on this subject, which was considered as an etiquette belonging to their places, and was therefore admitted; but it was well understood that no attempt would be made to speak in his defence.

Judge then how the French were astounded when they heard some distinguished Englishmen extolling Napoleon the Great, which they did in the French language, but sometimes in English phraseology; and the Parisians, who like better to laugh than to be angry, occasionally avenged themselves by citing pleasantly, in different companies, these neologisms in their English idiom. How, indeed, forbear a sickly smile when we hear newly-arrived strangers, after rolling lightly along the high road in their travelling carriages, having lolled in a box at the opera, walked through the gallery of the museum, and eat ices at Tortoni's, gravely assert, that there is no public misery in France, and that all is well and prosperous. The French are the same people, in one respect, as in the days of Mazarin—they will bear everything, but they *will* laugh.

At the time of Napoleon's return from Moscow, after the first burst of their indignation had subsided, one of the amusements of society was inventing or imagining caricatures, which no one dared to trace, but which were described in company as if they really existed. I remember one represented the entry of the French Army at Moscow. They were seen advancing towards the gate, which was thrown open, and where stood a Cossack to give them admission, as if it had been the door of a spectacle. The Cossack had a label on his breast, on which was written, "*Entrez, entrez, Messieurs—on ne payera qu'en sortant,*"

But to return to our narrative.—The allies were now in peaceable possession of Paris. An English and Prussian camp were formed close to each other in the Champs Elysées, and the white English tents made a very picturesque appearance among the trees. Here I saw, what to others appeared an army of foreigners, my own countrymen, and heard them talking familiarly my own language. I could not resist holding discourse with these Waterloo heroes, and I hope my French friends will forgive me if I felt a little proud of being an English-woman. Several Parisian ladies, who were parading in the walk, spoke to the sentinels in their lisping English, and were sometimes answered, by the smiling soldier, with "Eh, Ma'am?" for not one word did he comprehend, of his awn language, pronounced with a foreign accent.

In the meantime, the Legislative Body continued its labours upon the new constitution, and a Bill of Rights, in conformity to the example of the English at the *epocha* of their revolution. A deputy had some days before been denounced, by one of his colleagues, for having written and distributed a pamphlet, in which, said his accuser, "he had the infamy to abandon the cause of liberty, and recommend the return of the Bourbons." It was proposed to send him to a madhouse, as being the only place fitted for such an excess of alienation. This curious motion was made in a moment of effervescence after hearing the report of the commissaries sent to the army, who appeared to have cried, "*Vive Napoléon deux!*"

This cry, which they misnamed the cry of liberty, was re-vociferated by the Jacobins of the assembly; and in the fanaticism of the moment it was proposed to send the offending Bourbonist to Charenton, from which, however, he was saved by the inviolability of his character as deputy.

The debates of the Lower Chamber had grown more violent in proportion to the approach of danger; and while the cannon of the besiegers were sounding in the ears of these legislators, they decreed that an address should be made to the allied powers, declaring that the Bourbons were rejected as the enemies of the French nation; that no proposition of peace, which should tend to the re-establishment of this family, would be either received or listened to, and that the French were resolved to perish rather than submit to such a yoke. This decree of the chamber was ordered to be distributed to the army.

The French Empire, which had for some days past extended only from Ville Juif to St. Cloud, the distance of Kensington from Bow Bridge, and had since been narrowed to the space between La Chapelle and Vaugirard, the distance of Mile End from Hyde Park Corner, was at this critical moment comprised in Paris, and all without the gates became the Kingdom of France.

The king had issued a proclamation, dated from Cambray, the 28th June, in which he had declared his intention to assemble the two chambers immediately. The assembly answered this menace by the promulgation of a Bill of Rights, and the new constitution.

The two hostile camps were now those of the Legislative Body and of St. Denis, near which the king resided. The allies of the Legislative Body, which had hitherto been the military, were now succeeded by the mob. These citizens of both sexes besieged the barriers on the inside, which were again closed, and molested and ill-treated all passengers who had not divested themselves of the white cockade. Crowds of citizens had gone to St. Denis to gaze on their returning monarch, and hail his approach, having their white cockades in their pockets, which they placed in their hats after passing the barrier, and some had neglected, or were unwilling, to divest themselves of this cherished symbol at their return. But at the confines of the French Empire they were severely punished for their temerity. A family of my acquaintance had visited St. Denis, decorated with white flowers and white cockades; they disdained to conceal them at their return, and the marks of their guilt were glaring. Their carriage was assailed by volleys of stones, and their ears by the cry of "Traiterous royalists! Hang them up, *à la lanterne!*" &c. The gentleman was already dragged from his carriage, when the national guard interposed, and saved him, his trembling wife, and daughter, from the further assaults of the populace.

This was the last day of the authority of the mob, who, fearless of the English or Prussian bayonets, were vociferous in their cries of "*No Bourbons! Vive la representation nationale! Vivent la liberté et le pain blanc.*"[7] While the king in his proclamation stated that he had re-entered France to make himself the mediator between the allied armies and

7. "My comrades," said one of the *fédérés*, who had been sent as spy to the enemies' camp, "We are ruined, and betrayed; no more white bread. They swear that we shall have nothing but black; I have seen it with my own eyes, it is also devilishly hard baked—*Vive la liberté, et le pain blanc!*" The terrified *fédéré* had seen the accustomed rations for the allied armies. The cry of the populace was thus changed for the better, since Liberty and white bread are more reasonable than Liberty and the emperor.

the French, the assembly decreed a commission of four deputies who were to repair to the headquarters of the sovereigns, with the declaration of the Chambers, and solicit these high and mighty powers to become the mediators between the French and Louis XVIII.

M. La Fayette, named member of this commission, assured the assembly, that in the three conferences held at Haguenau,[8] the commissaries had received repeated assurances, that the allies would not mingle themselves with the internal government. This diplomatic contest was however decided at Paris, with nearly as much promptitude as that of the field of Waterloo; for whilst the Chamber of Peers was listening to the report of the committee, on the declaration of that of the deputies, respecting the Bill of Rights; and this last chamber was pondering on the advantages of an hereditary peerage, as a part of the constitution; a message from the provisionally government was announced, which instructed them, that although the allied sovereigns had hitherto appeared undecided in the choice of a prince to take the crown of France, they had, on the preceding day, made a declaration by their ministers and generals, that all the sovereigns were engaged to replace Louis XVIII. on the throne;—that he was to make his immediate entry into the capital, and that the Tuileries were now in possession of the foreign troops.

In this state of things they add:

> We have nothing to do, but to offer our vows for the country; and as our deliberations are no longer free, we deem it our duty to separate.

The Chamber of Peers heard the sentence of the allied sovereigns, and withdrew drew from the Luxembourg in respectful silence; the Commons were not so disposed. They were hearing the report of the commission on some part of the constitution which they were about to frame, when the message of the commission of government interrupted the speaker at the tribune. The debate on the constitution was then resumed, and the orator terminated his speech, by citing, and applying to themselves the memorable words of Mirabeau in the assembly at Versailles. The assembly, finding the capital surrounded, had on the preceding day made a solemn declaration, which might be called its testament, to the French nation.[9] After a desultory discussion on their personal situation, the assembly adjourned their meeting to the

---

8. See Appendix 1.
9. See Appendix 2.

following morning at an early hour. The deputies repaired to the hall at eight in the morning, and found it surrounded by a considerable number of troops, who refused them entrance. They repaired to the house of their president, where they made the following protest.

Chamber of Representatives:
8th July, 1815, 10 o'clock in the morning.

In yesterday's sittings, on the message by which the commission of government gave notice that it had ceased its functions, the Chamber of Representatives passed to the order of the day. It continued afterwards its deliberations on the dispositions of the project of the Constitutional Act, the framing of which was expressly ordered by the French people; and when its sittings were suspended, it adjourned to this day, the 8th July, at eight in the morning.

In consequence of this adjournment, the members of the Chamber of Representatives repaired to the usual place of their assembly. But the gates of the palace being shut, the avenues guarded by a military force, and the officers who commanded it having declared, that they had a formal order to refuse the entrance of the palace:

The undersigned, members of the Chamber, have assembled at the house of M. Lanjuinais, their president, and there they have formed, and signed individually the present *procès-verbal*, to authenticate the above facts.

On the morning of July the 8th, Paris was destined to be again united to the kingdom of France. The tri-coloured flag, which had hitherto floated on all the towers and monuments of the capital, bidding defiance to the white flag, which waved upon the steeples of St. Denis, was now taken down, and replaced by the crested lily.

The entry of the king on this day was announced, but the public were left in uncertainty whether the entrance would take place by the gate of St. Denis, or the less frequented road which leads to the barrier of Clichy, All was doubtful, but the joy of the great majority of the citizens, who now rushed out in multitudes by the re-opened gates to hail their monarch, by whom they were received with tender sensibility. The Comte d'Artois, in his usual manner of saying something agreeable to those who approach him, told them, "*Mes amis, vous serez contens de nous.*" Already a revolution seemed to have taken place in the minds of the turbulent *fédérés* of the Fauxbourgs. They had not yet cried *"Vive le Roi!"*—but their vociferations were already tempered by the expressions, *"Les Bourbons sont de bonnes gens—Le roi est un brave homme—mais, Vive l'Empereur!"*

Louis XVIII. attended by the Comte d'Artois, the Duke of Berry, and a numerous and brilliant escort of regular troops, and of the National Guard, now reached again his capital. I had often witnessed imperial processions, composed of gay regiments of lancers with floating banners, groups of pages, plumed horses, and the imperial figure, often vainly soliciting applause. It is true that the journals the following day spoke of acclamations that had never been heard, and of transports that had never been felt. The public had also been always prepared by programmes for the order of the ceremony. At the entry of Louis XVIII. there was no programme, for there had been no preparation. The procession was less magnificent, but its accompaniments were far different. No—Bonaparte, in all the pride of his conquests, was never so welcomed!

The people, which, as the poet observes, are always the sight on these occasions, the people are moral machines, and have feelings which power can neither command nor control. Here was no *"mouth-homage which the poor heart would fain deny, but dares not"*—what passed was the pure effusion of real happiness, and nothing is so contagious as the sympathy of a great multitude—it was *"the joy of tears"*—the people wept—and their monarch also. As he passed along the *boulevards,* *"you would have thought the very windows spoke;"*—they were crowded with women dressed in white, and white handkerchiefs floated from thousands of fair hands.

The evening closed by what with great propriety may be called spontaneous illuminations, for nobody had thought of giving any general order to that purpose. But the people understood one another, and, as if it had been by the touch of some magical wand, all Paris was suddenly lighted up. Its poorest inhabitants had found something to spare for this demonstration of joy; and while the splendid hotels of the wealthy blazed with a profusion of light, the lonely chamber of the indigent was cheered also with the luxury of a taper. At night we saw upon the surrounding hills the fires of the English and Prussian camps, where cannon was fired at intervals; and those commanding sounds gave something of solemnity to the whole scene, and produced the effect of that instrument, whose deep, full base, strikes upon the ear at intervals, covering the light strains of the concert.

The celebration of this triumph was prolonged far beyond the day of the procession; and nothing was omitted to convince the king with what fond enthusiasm he was welcomed. No people understand better the demonstration of happiness than the French. Prolonged calamity has rendered them sometimes serious, sometimes even sorrowful, but their natural position is gaiety. The French manner of manifesting joy is always by dancing; a practice, by the way, not peculiar to this polished people, but common also to many transatlantic nations. The garden of the Tuileries, which had been entirely abandoned by the higher classes during the king's absence, was now thronged by elegant company. Ladies formed their own sets for country-dances, and bringing their own music with them, danced light as nymphs, and crowned with lilies, before the windows of the *château*; where the king stood, sometimes gracefully kissing his hand, and sometimes wiping his eyes, while he witnessed all these testimonies of enthusiastic affection.

LETTER 13

July, 1815.

While these joys and festivities exhilarated the people of Paris, he, who had once more yielded the throne of France to the race of its ancient kings, was hastening to seek security in another hemisphere. Two frigates were prepared for him in the River Charente; but when he arrived at Rochefort, it was blockaded by an English squadron, and therefore no hope of escape presented itself, but by seeking, to use the words of Mr. Pitt, "*the protection of a tempest.*" But a long dead calm prevailed. In vain Bonaparte invoked the winds, and accused the elements:—there was no storm but in his agitated bosom. It was observed that the spell was now broken by which he was once believed to have some kind of power, divine or infernal, which controlled the natural course of the weather. The times were past when the Parisians had often confidently exclaimed on a morning of festival, "*It rains, and is cloudy, but the sun will shine when the emperor appears.*"

At length, however, the gale freshened, and he eagerly inquired of the captain of the frigate, if this was the moment to escape? The captain answered that he was ready to obey his orders, and make the attempt, but hinted to him at the same time, that it was probable they should go up, or go down, pointing emphatically to the sky, and the water; by which he meant that they should be sunk, or blown up. Bonaparte loves life too well not to shrink from such an alternative. The English had subdued him by land—with how much reason might he deprecate their power on their own element? He had tried English valour, and felt its worth; he now resolved to appeal to English generosity. He opened a conference with the English commander of the station, and soon after, under the shelter of the white flag, steered his course towards the English frigate, and surrendered himself a prisoner.

Thus ends the political history of Napoleon Bonaparte; since on the distant and lonely rock, beat by all the waves of a vast ocean, whither he is now steering his course, he is no doubt separated for ever from public life; and although he is still condemned to suffer existence, he has bid a last farewell to the present generation, and may be said to belong already to history.

He leaves a name at which the world grew pale,
To point a moral, or adorn a tale.

You desire me to give you a sketch of the character of this extraordinary personage; but who at present can well acquit themselves of such a task?—We must leave him to posterity—Time will place his figure in the point of view, and at the proper distance, to become a study for mankind. At present, and above all in this country, we have seen him too near. We have felt his influence too powerfully. His portentous shadow has crossed every path of private life, and even the persons whom he has not destroyed, he has appalled and stunned; as the wind of a cannon will lay prostrate those whom the ball has never touched. But if we leave to future times to seize the pencil, and draw the bold lights and shades of this tremendous picture, we may now sketch some of the minuter, scattered traits of character, which mark so memorable a personage, before they fade from the remembrance.

The great sages of antiquity had each their Demon; Bonaparte's Demon was his *destin*. He acted as if he thought himself under the immediate influence of some sort of super-human power; and in the commission of the greatest injustice, seemed to persuade himself that it was so ordained by fate. His belief in his own superiority over other mortals was so rooted in his mind, that he welcomed and rewarded the public declaration that the care of this nether world was confided to him, and that "*God had created him, and rested from his labours;*" as also the assertion that he was the Vicegerent of the Divinity on earth. He deemed it favourable to his views to encourage all extravagant ideas with respect to himself. Every age has its superstitions. The priests of the Egyptian Jupiter hailed Alexander as the son of that divinity. It was the belief of the dark ages that mankind were subjected to planetary influence; and one of our poets has good-humouredly framed this apology for one part of the creation;

When poor weak women go astray,
Their stars are more in fault than they.

But the stars have been long since exonerated from those unde-
served reproaches; and we are now told by the physiology of the day,
that being well-born is a much happier incident than it was believed
to be by the Romans, although they considered this circumstance as a
good cause of rejoicing. When any new enormity of the emperor became the subject of conversation, I had long observed that one person
of my acquaintance shook his head, like Lord Burleigh in the *Critic*,
but said nothing. I was curious to know the opinion of this gentleman,
who is by profession a more accurate observer of human heads than
others. This celebrated physiologist said:

When I beheld this man ten years since in Italy, I augured ill of
his destiny. His head partakes too much of the organisation of
the tyger and the peacock; it is cruel and climbing.

Was Bonaparte ill-born, or unhappily organised; or did the cruel
and climbing qualities of his mind contribute to produce this formation? This point I leave to the metaphysician and the anatomist. Some
persons believed that he was in a state of habitual insanity, with a few
lucid intervals. It is very complaisant morality that tends to diminish
our horror of guilt, by attributing its excesses to insanity. If Bonaparte was mad, there was too much *"method in his madness"* to exempt
him from being classed among great and extraordinary criminals. He
indeed occasionally displayed something like minor fits of madness,
towards his ministers and generals; the former of whom were bound
to think him mad, when he answered their observations by a kick, or
a blow, while the latter escaped this imperial mode of reply, because he
prudently observed, that, like himself, they wore a sword. His orders
sometimes appeared to issue from the fumes of the tripod; and he was
subject to fits of epilepsy.

The obdurate cruelty with which, after a battle, he would walk
over the field and count the number of the slain, was too long forgotten by the French, in the splendour of his victories; and the excess of
his vanity was too long pardoned, because his triumphs were shared
by the *Great Nation*, the country that gave laws to Europe. Bonaparte
despised mankind in general, at which mankind has no right to be
offended, for he had marked it from a sorry point of view; but he had

the most decided contempt for what is called the people, especially if they were considered as presuming to interfere with any part of the government. I remember being told several years since, by some deputies from the Helvetic Republic, that in a conference at the Tuileries, he proposed a regulation, which they replied that the people would never suffer to be executed. He said:

The people! Who are they? What do they understand?—they are only fit to make shoes; (citing the Latin proverb).

Although Bonaparte appeared to court the government of the United States, on account of the increasing hostile dispositions between that government and the English, and which he hoped to fan into a flame, his expressions of hatred against the United States were occasionally violent and insulting. The ministers of that power happily escaped the smart of his invectives, since most commonly they did not understand the language of the country to which they were sent as the representatives of their own.[10] This, however, was not the case with Mr. Barlow, the last minister but one. His long residence in France had made him not only acquainted with its language, but with the state-practice of its chief. This minister, distinguished as a man of letters, had also been long known for his attachment to the principles that governed his own country. He was decidedly averse to the war that then menaced America and England, and which it was evident Bonaparte wished to promote.

The emperor was alternately flattering and stern. The minister was unbending. The emperor was at length made acquainted with the minister's private opinion of his imperial policy. Required with other ministers to follow Napoleon as far as Wilna, Mr. Barlow was compelled to pass the Polish deserts in the most severe rigour of winter, and died at the village of N———, the victim of what he deemed his diplomatic duty.

Bonaparte had a great anxiety not only to spread his name throughout the world, but to learn what the world said of him, particularly the English. He did not understand English, but he had a board of translation, and was regularly served each morning with the daily London papers, done into French. He affected to be indifferent whether he

10 "I have the honour," said an American minister to Bonaparte, "*de vous présenter un respectable marchand Améericain.*" The minister meant to introduce a merchant; but the term *marchand* denoted a shopkeeper.—Bonaparte, extremely offended, made no answer, but turning to his master of ceremonies, ordered him to inform the American minister, that he received no *marchands* at the Tuileries.

found praise or invectives; when a paragraph in an English newspaper struck him as being particularly virulent, he sent it to be re-translated by another person; and if he found it still more poignant than the first translator had made it, and which sometimes happened, he reprimanded the poor wight for his culpable scrupulosity not to wound the imperial feelings, which was the excuse generally offered. The translators learnt at last to give every epithet its due signification, and even to overcharge it.

Bonaparte considered the English newspapers as good as diplomatic dispatches, and containing more accurate information of the state of Europe than the reports of his emissaries at foreign courts. His translators made such strange blunders in the transcript of names, that he often himself collated the translation with the original. In one of these surveys, my name fell under his notice, prefixed to a few verses I had written on the peace at Amiens. He inquired why they were not translated? The translator, with whom I was acquainted, answered, that this had been omitted in conformity to his orders to translate nothing of literature, or poetry, in which his name was not mentioned. But could this be possible?—An *Ode on Peace*, without any mention of the Great Pacificator! *Le Grand Pacificateur!*—words, which now resounded throughout all France; words that were engraved on marble in palaces, and stuck up below his bust, placed as a signpost at the door of every hedge-alehouse on the highway.

The ode was translated; and if the First Consul was angry at what was omitted, he was far more irritated at what he found: this was the epithet of *subject* waves, applied to England

And thou, loved Britain, my parental isle,
Secure, encircled by thy subject waves, &c.

This was touching a jarring string indeed this was declaring myself of the faction of sea-despots. It was almost treason: but I had friends at court, and therefore escaped with a slight punishment, inflicted a few months after by the prefect of police, who arrested me, and my whole family, on pretext of examining my papers; from which ordeal I came out triumphant, having been detained a prisoner only twenty-four hours.

Napoleon considered the police of his own newspapers as a matter of high importance. When he was in Paris, the official paper, before it was struck off, underwent his inspection, and in the course of the impression often received imperial corrections. He was himself a contributor; his style is very distinguishable, and some of his notes are extremely curious. He affected to protect science and letters. This protection was commonly extended to persons whose mediocrity stood in need of it; small men of letters, by whom it was repaid with interest. There were, indeed, also a few men of distinguished genius, whose approbation of his measures had led him to name them to eminent posts.[11] Bonaparte had once been very intimately acquainted with M. Ducis, the present father of French poetry, and who has introduced *Hamlet*, *Othello*, and *Macbeth*, on the French stage.

M. Ducis had approved Bonaparte while he thought him the friend of his country, but refused all further communion with him when he became its oppressor. The Muses in France have as little of the wisdom of this world as in other countries, and understand no better the art of being rich. Bonaparte knew that the fortune of M. Ducis was in "a poetical posture," and he offered him the place of senator, which includes a very considerable salary. Ducis rejected the place as being unfit for a poet. Bonaparte would have decorated him with the Legion of Honour; again Ducis refused. Irritated at this obstinacy, the emperor meditated to avenge the insult, when he was pacified, by some of M. Ducis's friends, who excused him on the score of his drooping age. I visited this virtuous old man, the last of the Romans, in his retreat. He was surrounded by his books, and did not appear to regret the wealth and honours he had rejected. He was presented, not long since, to the king, who addressed the poet in a citation from his own works.

The tragic talents of M. Ducis lead me to the recollection of an anecdote relating to the theatre.

Bonaparte had in the early time of his government expelled the turbulent *tribunate*, and reduced the legislature to a silent vote; but there was still one authority in the state which his power was unable to control; a faction which had hitherto mocked his efforts. This was the faction of the tragic poets, Corneille, Racine, Crebillon, &c. The people, amidst the suppression of their political institutions, and other violations of independence, could still repair to the theatre, and avenge themselves of Bonaparte in the persons of the Caesars, the Neros, the Phocases, of the French stage. The people had in long tradition, for an

---

11. He was, however, sometimes tired with excess of servility, and answered one of the *litterati*, who recommended another, because he was of an ancient and noble family, by saying, peevishly, "*Laissez-nous, au moins, la république des lettres!*"—Leave us, at least, the republic of letters!

hundred years past, applauded certain fine passages filled with horror of tyranny, or swelling sentiments of freedom; but these passages were now waited for, and hailed with such excess of applause, such a transport of admiration, that the government felt itself insulted.

The actors, who were not displeased at the popular enthusiasm, and who no doubt attributed to themselves some share of the applause, strove to earn it by acquitting themselves well of their respective parts, and played the tyrant and usurper most maliciously. It became indispensable to stop this outrage on imperial feelings. The representatives of past despots, and of captive princesses, were ordered to appear at the *prefecture's* of police, and were accused of acting the forbidden passages with more emphasis than usual. The accusation was a delicate matter, since it implied a certain consciousness that there was "something rotten in the State of Denmark;" and one of the tragical queens haughtily answered, that she wondered how any one dared to hint at such guilty applications, and that she considered them as treason against the emperor. The actors refuted the charge of saying more than was set down for them, by an appeal to the prompter's book. They were dismissed with orders to "mouth it less," and the poets were found to be the chiefs of the conspiracy.

Their persons were beyond the reach of imperial resentment, but they did not escape punishment; being condemned to a revision of the most brilliant passages of their productions, This revision was confided to M. Esmenard, who had too much poetical taste and talent not to tremble at this sacrilegious commission. But the emperor insisted, and he was compelled to submit. He gave me a ludicrous account of his association and clossetings with Bonaparte, in this murder of the classic poets. Many an important dispatch was laid aside to weigh the value of an hemistich; and imperial rage against the present sovereigns of Europe was forgotten in contrivance to justify some Roman or Asiatic despot, who had fallen under the displeasure of Corneille.

The public sought in vain to recognise their old acquaintances;

> *Qui, de simple soldat, à l'empire élevé,*
> *Ne l'a que par le crime acquis, et conservé;*
> *Et comme il n'a semé qu'épouvante, et qu'horreur,*
> *Il ne recueille enfin que trouble, et que terreur.*
> ✶✶✶✶✶✶
> *Tyran, descends du trône, et fais place à ton maître!*

The public deserted for a while the theatre, and waited the return of departed spirits.

But you tell me that "Napoleon has performed one great act of wide extended charity, which covers many a transgression; he has decreed the abolition of the Slave Trade." And do you really imagine that he would have adhered to this decree longer than he found it expedient to flatter, in this manner, the people of England, with whom he was assured it would render him popular? Do you seriously believe in his tender compassion towards the African race, and figure him fraternising with the friends of that oppressed part of our species?—associating his power with their humanity?—a compact of philanthropy between Napoleon Bonaparte, Wilberforce, and Clarkson? I see the first-mentioned of the high contracting parties smiling with pity at his two allies; their wild theories of universal benevolence, and their insensate practice of living only for others.

No, no; Bonaparte would soon have dissolved this partnership with virtue. To become the deliverer of one part of mankind would have been too pure a glory for him who had so long oppressed the other. He deserved not the honours of such a triumph. But at the moment in which I am writing, this great work of mercy is accomplished. The Slave Trade is abolished by the French government; that horrible traffic, which seemed an evil too much in the sad catalogue of human miseries, exists no longer; and while European mothers press to their bosoms the children they no longer fear to lose, the poor African mother, to whom nature has given the same instinctive tenderness, will now be spared also the pangs of maternal desperation.

Bonaparte had at one period so established his power, that he, as well as his flatterers, deemed himself the irresistible, the omnipotent. He had conquered almost all the nations of Europe; he had trampled on all institutions that were not his own. There was but one power that resisted him; one power that rebuked his genius, and baffled all his efforts to obtain universal empire. He learnt that India was the source of this power. He cries:

Let us attack England at the source. Think nothing gained, while aught remains. The English are masters at sea, but the dry land is ours. If we cannot stab England to the heart at once, we will disable her by cutting off her limbs.

The Macedonian conqueror had penetrated to the Indies with only thirty thousand men; Bonaparte could surely reach the Ganges with at least ten times that number.

When nothing more was intended than an European irruption, Bonaparte had no counsel to take. The continent was to him a high road unencumbered by obstacles; and Munich, Berlin, and Vienna, were regular stages of the journey. The sea alone resisted his dominion. He was yet sovereign only of the dry ground; and overland to India was now the secret order of the day. It was yet secret, because the military expeditions to the east had been hitherto profitable only to *savans*, to the engravers of charts and picturesque views, and to those who were employed at Paris in writing the histories of the victories in Egypt for the magnificent edition of these exploits which was there about to appear. The public were therefore not yet admitted to anticipate this new and glorious enterprise, which was to emancipate Europe and the seas.

In the prosecution of this plan, difficulties might be expected to occur on the road, which Alexander had not encountered. Some changes in the weapons of war had taken place since the time of that hero, when the art of bringing armies into the field, in order to stand like machines, and be mowed down by artillery, was yet unknown. Cannon was now become the chief instrument of destruction, and must therefore be placed in the first line of offensive apparatus. The mode of its conveyance, so many thousand miles, presented some difficulties. The master of the ordnance was consulted; I saw daily this respectable old general, having lived some years in his hotel. His military and his civic virtues had procured him the esteem of the emperor, whom he was too honest to flatter, or to mislead. I observed him one evening exploring my library with some marks of impatience at not finding what he sought. When his suite of officers were gone, he drew his chair towards the fire, and, as I supposed, to finish a story of the preceding evening. He saw the emperor every day, and I asked what was passing at the Tuileries?

> The emperor has given me a new employment, he orders me to be a *savant*. I wish you to lend me what you have of the geography and the manners of the east.

Of the manners of the east I had nothing more modern than the *Arabian Nights*; with its geography I was better stored. But there was one great obstacle to this imperial adventure which it was essential to remove. Alexander had conquered Thrace, Illyria, and by the ruins of Thebes had secured the silence of Greece, before he crossed into Asia. It was necessary for Bonaparte to assure himself of the neutrality at

102

least, if not of the alliance of the modern Alexander of the polar world. This sovereign had once thought Bonaparte a man of honour, just and tenacious of his word; he had made peace with him, and treaties. The Emperor of Russia had now learnt the true character of Bonaparte. Alexander could no longer be deceived, he must be subdued.

The result of this war of passage sickened Napoleon of Indian expeditions, dimmed his star, broke all his spells, destroyed all his witcheries, and brought the Russian armies into his capital.

This Indian project has eventually led him, who was about to style himself not merely the emperor of the west, but who probably hoped to be addressed in the language of oriental salutation, as Brother of the Moon, or Cousin of the Stars, to that little speck which rises in a distant ocean, where its waves approach the confines of the civilized world.

Du midi jusqu'à l'Ours on vantait ce monarque
Qui remplit tout le Nord de tumulte et de sang:
Il fuit; sa gloire tombe, et le Destin lui marque
Son véritable rang.

Ce n'est plus ce héros guidé par la Victoire,
Par qui tons les guerriers allaient être effacés;
C'est un nouveau Pyrrhus, qui va grossir l'histoire
Des fameux insensés.
—Jean Baptiste Rousseau. *Ode X.*

You ask me what will be the fate of France? I remember being affected by a few simple words in the *Beggar Girl*; (a novel, by the way, with which perhaps I was more pleased than I strictly ought to have been, because the scene is laid in Scotland, the country of my mother, and its personages speak in Scotch accents, which are ever music to my ear:) I remember the Beggar Girl exultingly exclaims, when she approaches the castle of Dening-Court, "I feel as if at last at last—I was going home!"—Are the French people, after all the mazy wanderings of the Revolution, are they approaching an asylum like Dening-Court; are they going home at last?—This is indeed a momentous question. It is not made by me, as perhaps it may be by yourself, in the spirit of speculative investigation; to me it comprehends all that can awaken solicitude, all that can interest the heart; all chance of personal tranquillity towards the evening of a stormy life, and all hope of felicity for the objects most dear to me, and to whom life is opening. France is to me also the country of my friends—of persons endeared to me by the tie of common suffering.

We have passed through the tempest, to use the words of M. de Boufflers, "*sous la même parapluie.*" How should I have lived so many years among the French without loving that amiable people, to apply the term in their own sense, who so well know the art of shedding a peculiar charm over social life! How much better than others they understand the secret of being happy! happy at a cheap rate, and without being too difficult, and too disdainful as we are in England about the conditions; while they bear misfortunes with a cheerful equanimity, which, if it does not deserve the proud name of philosophy, is of far more general use; the former being common property, belonging to all, and not, like the latter, the partial fortune of an enlightened few.

I am persuaded that the experience acquired by the French nation during their long and stormy Revolution, will not be lost. Their political vanity and presumption required a tremendous lesson. They have passed through many phases, from the wildest anarchy to the most oppressive despotism; and they now really know what is *not* freedom. They seek repose, but it must be repose under the safe shelter of liberty. To use the language of the Duke d'Otrante, in his letter to the Duke of Wellington:

> They pretend not, they pretend not to more liberty than that of England, but they seek to be as free.

You will not, I am sure, answer, as I have heard some of our countrymen:

> Liberty for England, but arbitrary government for the continent.

England need not fear the rivalship of France in its constitutional freedom. It will be some time before the French reach your practical science on this subject. They have indeed already lost some of that vanity of knowledge, which is only found in the first steps of its acquirement, because we look back on the time when we knew nothing. The French were too proud of their ABC liberty; they feel now that the alphabet is only the rudiment of science. They have learnt the table of contents of liberal principles, and they will at last comprehend the whole volume.

The Revolution, amidst all its abuses and its crimes, has shed a new ray of light upon France, and it were vain to expect that the French will shut their minds against it, and prefer the darkness of ignorance.

The eternal principles of liberty are independent of the purposes to which they have been made subservient. What is good in those principles is unperishable, and what has been evil in their application will be transitory. But time has no sponge that can wipe from the memory of the French the great event of the Revolution, and restore prejudices that are swept away, ideas that are eradicated, manners that are changed, and affections that are extinct. The spirit of constitutional representation is abroad, and will walk the world. Louis XVIII. has no reason to fear its energies, for he will be strong only in its strength.

"*J'aimerais bien*," said a man of the Fauxbourg St. Antoine, to a member of the Convention, who was haranguing the people in the time of terror, "*J'aimerais bien, Citoyen Représentant, une liberté libre.*" Oh, may such liberty belong to France! May that noble country, which has long been so brilliant abroad, and so oppressed at home,—so erect, and so prostrate—at length revive from the pressure of her unexampled calamities, and take her august place among the nations! Yes, she will now form new combinations of glory, and seek new objects of activity for her ardent spirit, in the cultivation of the fine arts, so well suited to her elegant genius, in the discoveries of science, and the researches of truth; and her energies, no longer wasted on the crusades of ambition, but directed towards intellectual attainments, in eternal alliance with the first feelings of our nature, will no doubt, from the prevailing influence of such a country as France, have a powerful tendency towards the general amelioration of the human race.

LETTER 14

October, 1815.

You accuse me of having closed my sketch of passing events too rapidly. Is it my fault?—I believed that I had brought you to the conclusion of the eventful drama,—the fall of the usurper, and the return of the exiled monarch to the palace of his ancestors. I knew not that we had only reached the fourth act of the piece, and that the allies had new scenes to perform before they would drop the curtain on the events of war.

The moderation of the allied powers last year when Europe was in arms at the gates of Paris, with all the feelings of the wrongs it had sustained, and with all the rights of the conqueror, would, it was believed, serve as a precedent for the conduct of the allies in this second conquest of the capital of France.

It was fondly imagined by the French, that European politics were changed for ever; and that the vulgar ambition of darker ages had given place to that magnanimity worthy of our enlightened times, and confirming all the beautiful systems of human perfectibility. All that had passed the last year had served to establish this opinion. Satisfied with the glory of having overthrown the tyrant of Europe, and compelled France to relinquish the immense territories she had conquered, all further restitution seemed forgotten; and the only object in Paris, that had not been respected, was the statue of Napoleon, which was quietly taken down from the column of victory in the Place Vendôme; while the monument itself remained untouched. Upon the whole, with the exception of a few provinces, which the allied armies had traversed, France had suffered but little from their first invasion; and it was generally believed that, having once more accomplished their great purpose, they would depart in peace.

This, however, was not precisely the design of at least a part of the allies. The Prussians, since their last visit, had found time to reflect on their adventures. They had indeed regained their old territory with considerable augmentations; they had nothing farther to apprehend from the conqueror of Jena and Berlin; but they now reflected that they had been too moderate in the conditions of the treaty,—that they had in the last visit left the Parisians too many trophies of victory, and also that they had yet to retaliate on them a few of the many enormities which the French had committed in Prussia.

The first patriotic project of vengeance that occupied Prince Blücher was that of blowing up the bridge of Jena; the execution of which attempt was prevented by the interference of the King of Prussia, whose moderation and mildness of character are well known. The next menace of General Blücher was that of sending a considerable number of Paris bankers and merchants to Prussian fortresses, unless they paid, in twenty-four hours, the fifth part of the hundred millions imposed on the city of Paris. These projects, though not executed, were considered by the troops as intimations that their own excesses or extravagancies would be treated with indulgence.

A great part of these troops were of the *landwehr*, or Prussian levy in mass; they were in general very poor, and their poverty might excuse pillage: but another part of this army consisted of professors and students, who, with noble devotedness to the cause of their country, had made this crusade as volunteers. The *landwehr* committed great acts of violence, but these armed doctors exercised a new kind vengeance. A Frenchman might be robbed, he might suffer even indignities

with patience; but to be compelled to listen to the discourses of professors and students, who assured him, like the executioners of Don
Carlos, that they had come only for his good; who would persuade
him of the vast superiority of the German over the French nation; of
the propriety of detaching from France one or two of its provinces on
the Rhine, with other topics of similar import—this was a refinement
in cruelty beyond the rights of war. The bad French and worse logic
of those war-doctors were alike insufferable to French ears and French
vanity: the tortured Gaul exclaimed in piteous accents, "Rob me, if
you please; shoot me, if you will; but spare me your harangues."

The Prussians were thus become the objects of general hatred.
There might, indeed, be some doubt whether they were more de-
tested than the Wirtemberghers, the Badois, and the Bavarians. The
causes of this hatred against the Prussians, must be placed to the exercise of that spirit of vengeance to which this army too readily abandoned itself; and which was not always tempered by chiefs to whom
we should have attributed more philosophic ideas. We may at the
same time observe, that those who suffer are usually unjust. Marshal
Blücher was often accused unjustly by the French, because he was the
commander-in-chief, and perhaps, sometimes, because he bore the
German name which they could most easily articulate. The Generals
Bülow, Zeithen, Tauenzien, and some others, always interposed their
authority to prevent the outrages of their troops.

Order was still preserved in Paris; but the inhabitants without the
walls, and the country around, were left to feel the full vengeance of
a licentious soldiery, who, by the most wanton spoliations, taught the
French what the Prussians had undergone from the former visits of
their countrymen. The poor peasant was too often the victim of this
vengeance; the remains of his last year's harvest was devoured. The
pleasure that the husbandman feels in watching the alternate descent
of the fostering showers, and the vivid sunbeams that ripen the fruits
of the fields, was here lost in the cruel apprehension, that in whatever
disposition he had sown, he should not reap in joy. The soldier eyed
askance the corn as it ripened, and the grape as it swelled: while the
desponding owner, instead of thanking heaven, as usual, for its bounties, turned no eyes to heaven, unless to invoke its vengeance on Prussian soldiery.

The Parisians themselves received occasional lessons from these
invaders. An old countess, in the Fauxbourg St. Germain, welcomed
with politeness a Prussian officer who was quartered on her house.

Invited to dinner at the usual time, he ordered that it might be ready at an earlier hour, having asked some brother-officers to dine with him; and throwing himself at the same time with his dirty boots on one of the blue silk canopies. He went out, and returned alone.

The dinner was served. He found the first course detestable, and threw the successive plates to which he was helped on the floor. Shewn to his apartments on the second storey, he refused to occupy them, and ordered those of the first floor to be prepared for him, though told that they were inhabited by the mistress of the house. After committing a number of other extravagancies, such as smoking in the lady's *boudoir*, he took possession of her chamber. His servants, and dogs, having retired to the apartments prepared for their master, the lady of the house was obliged to accommodate herself with a room in the attic storey.

The next morning she was summoned to attend the officer, which she did with trembling, expecting to receive some new insult or humiliation. The countess was astonished at her reception. The Prussian led her gallantly to a seat, and placed himself beside her. "You have no doubt, madam," he said, "been shocked at my behaviour in your house. I marked your astonishment at my insolence in spoiling your silk furniture, scattering fragments of your viands on the floor, smoking in your *boudoir*, turning you out of your apartments, and other extravagancies. You no doubt thought me a barbarian." The countess did not seem disposed to deny the allegation. "Madam, you have a son in Prussia?"

She started, and her eyes filled with tears, "I had a son, sir, but I fear he has perished."

"Do you recognise this writing?" said the officer, shewing her the cover of a letter.

"Yes, sir, it is the last letter I wrote to my son, I have received no answer."

"Madam, I am no barbarian; I have acted a part, and fulfilled a duty enforced on me by filial tenderness. I almost hate myself for having acted it so well. What I have made you suffer for these last few hours, your son inflicted on my palsied mother for several months. I will distress you no longer—your son is alive In one of the last skirmishes he was wounded dangerously—I saved him from the fury of our soldiers—My mother provided for his safety You will soon receive him to your arms. *Adieu*, madam, I quit your house; I have preserved your son, and I have avenged my mother."

In the country through which the English were dispersed no complaint was heard. They paid for everything they demanded from the cottager; they laboured at the harvest, gathered in the fruits of the orchards, and busied themselves in the occupation of rural industry. "Happy," said the peasants, "the country where the English are quartered!"

The Austrians and Russians conducted themselves with a becoming spirit of moderation. The former had not been goaded on to revenge by outrages such as the Prussians had sustained; and the Emperor of Russia had too liberal a mind to seek retaliation for the flames of Moscow, in the destruction of Paris.

In the meantime, if France, in the possession of the allies, was no longer at war, it could not be said to be at peace. We heard of nothing but attacks, skirmishes, and sieges. In vain the white flag waved over the ramparts of fortified towns, and in vain the besieged demanded to surrender to their legitimate sovereign, the King of France.

Paris itself, though spared the worst evils of war, wears still the aspect of a conquered city, guarded by foreign troops at all its gates; foreign troops posted at every bridge; and cannon, which seemed as if it were pointed at the palace of the Tuileries. The Bois de Boulogne, the Hyde Park of Paris, may now be termed rather a desert than a royal domain. We might almost imagine ourselves in the wilds of America, amidst huts framed of logs and branches, with the ground cleared around them, and nothing left but the stumps of trees, marking where they once grew. The walks, formerly crowded with splendid equipages of the gay and great, have lost their shade and their visitors, and are transformed into streets of tents; here and there a tall withered stalk of a tree remains, and serves, like old Lasune's house,[12] as a rubbing-post for the cattle.

I sometimes take a walk in this wood, and sometimes visit the English camp formed at Neuilly, in what was once the park of *her*, who was once the Queen of Naples. Could Madame Murat, in any moment when fancy plays her wildest vagaries, have ever dreamt of so strange a transformation? Would she have believed any wizard who had whispered in her ear, that his magical rod would one day change her beautiful and splendid pavilion into lodgings and eating-rooms for English officers; and that her charming park, with its terrace gently sloping towards the Seine, would be covered with soldiers' tents?—the trees cut down to serve the English for fuel, and the Austrians, who

12. Julia de Roubigné.

have no tents, for huts; the ground roughened by the wheels of artillery and army-waggons; numerous camp-fires lighted in holes dug in the smooth lawns, and clouds of steam issuing from a thousand boiling black kettles?

While I was one day observing the occupations of the busy camp, an epitome of the busy world, I heard at a little distance approaching music; the sounds were slow and solemn. I soon perceived a funeral procession advancing towards us; it was the burial of a young Scotch soldier; his sword, and hat, with a band of Scotch plaid, which conjured up many a recollection in my mind, were placed upon his coffin, which was borne along by his comrades, of whom a considerable number preceded and followed their dead companion. The band of the regiment played the music of the Hundred and Fourth psalm; and two drums, with a deep, continued rolling sound, formed the base.

As the procession passed, the noisy camp became suddenly still; every soldier uncovered his head, and those on duty at the posts presented their arms. I saw some of those brave fellows wipe their eyes. This was not the moment when the soldier, in the fury of battle, rushes on death, as if it were some new transport to die—careless of himself, and scorning even to lament his friend—this was the calm hour of milder emotion, and the heart had leisure to feel—this was death, but not under the form in which the brave are accustomed to despise it. They were going, in a foreign land, to render the last duties to their comrade, who would see his home no more!

I figured to myself the poor dying young man, recollecting, perhaps, in his latest moments, his cottage at the foot of a Scotch mountain, and lamenting that he was going to be laid at such sad distance from what Ossian calls *the rock of his rest.* I followed him to his grave in the churchyard of Neuilly—and listened with emotion to the burial service, which was read by the chaplain of the regiment, in English. After a long lapse of time passed in a foreign country, who can hear unmoved, a religious ceremony performed in that language in which the first prayer of childhood has been uttered, and the first feeling of devotion impressed upon the heart!

Letter 15

October, 1815.

The period was now arrived when a new storm no less horrible than unforeseen brooded over Paris. It appears that the allied powers, amidst those rapid and brilliant successes, which in the year 1814 had rendered them masters of the capital, had not overlooked the *chefs-d'oeuvre* of art which had been wrested from their respective countries By the right of conquest.

The allied sovereigns, when they visited the Gallery of the Louvre, beheld pictures and statues once their own, and saw them noted in the preface of the catalogues, sold at the door, as the fruit of French victories. The Prussians had not failed to observe that pictures which had decorated the bedchamber of their beautiful and lamented queen were then placed in the royal apartments of the palace of St. Cloud.

There was also a statue in the museum which was known by the name of the Ganymede of Sans Souci. This statue was of bronze, and of the most beautiful workmanship; it was no less perfect than the Belvidere Apollo, and held that reputation in the north. It was erroneously called a Ganymede, the pose of the arms leading to this mistake, but it is a gladiator giving thanks to the gods for a victory just obtained.

The Prussians demanded, in 1814, the restoration of this statue, of two pieces by Corregio, and the pictures of St. Cloud, which had been taken from the apartment of their queen.

The restitution of these objects became the subject of a most fastidious negotiation between M. Blacas and the ministers of Austria and Prussia. It had been agreed at the peace of Paris, that nothing should be touched that was then exhibited in the Museum, and M. Blacas wished to extend this article to all the paintings in the royal palaces. The negotiation failed. Paris preserved its statues and pictures, and the Prussians their regrets at not having regained the trophies stripped from their queen's apartments.

The allied armies, in 1815, again crowned the hills around Paris, and again a capitulation was asked and granted. The Provisionary Government demanded that the Museum should remain untouched. The allied generals wrote with a pencil, on the margin of this article, *non accordé*, (not granted). This refusal, it appears, did not arise so much from any decision taken with respect to the Museum by the Duke of Wellington, who would not prejudge the question, but because General Blücher, supported by the public opinion of his country, had, in his own mind, determined upon taking. The article on the respect to be paid to public and private property was loosely worded. The Provisionary Government were, perhaps, not sorry to have left room for misinterpretation, since the surrender of Paris was unavoidable. The allies assert that their respect for the monuments of the arts could never be justly applied to the retaking of objects which had at first been seized by violence.

General Blücher, immediately upon his entrance into Paris, sent a letter to M. Denon, the Director of the Museum, demanding not only the objects of the last year's negotiation with M. Blacas, but what was also in the museum. M. Denon answered, that it was an affair which must be negotiated with his government, and that he would not give them up. M. Denon was arrested during the night by twenty men, and was threatened to be sent to the fortress of Graudentz in West Prussia.

From this argument there was no appeal. The objects demanded were delivered. This surrender was made in due order, and the Gladiator, the two pictures of Corregio, and some valuable pieces of the old German school, were carefully packed up by the persons employed at the museum. This would have been but a trifling loss had not the King of Prussia taken not only what belonged to Potzdam and Berlin, but also to Cologne and Aix la Chapelle, countries on this side of the Rhine, and therefore not in his possession at that period, on the pretext that these objects belonged to the cathedral, and the municipality of those towns.

The public mind again became tranquil; it was asserted these acts of Prussian violence had neither the assent of the Emperor of Russia, nor of the Duke of Wellington, and it was currently believed that they had condemned these measures.

Two months had now passed when the Gallery of the Louvre was menaced from another quarter. The King of the Belgic Provinces now united to Holland had published a Constitution in the modern style, that is, on free and liberal principles. It was understood that it had met with a general acceptance, for who would refuse the blessings of liberty? The acceptance, however, was not so cordial as had been generally believed. There was a numerous and respectable class of the inhabitants of those provinces who were not eager to adopt strange doctrines, or suffer them to be adopted by those under their influence.

The Catholic clergy, in that country, had displayed some energy twenty years since, when, threatened with liberal principles, they roused the faithful into insurrection against such innovations by their then lawful sovereign. The Emperor Joseph the Second, who will be ranked in the class of philosophic princes, was studious to introduce what he deemed free and liberal principles among his Belgian subjects. But the clergy saw in toleration the destruction of religion, and in liberal principles the subversion of the privileges of the church. They resisted, with force of arms, those dangerous tenets, and framed for themselves a government exempt from such political heresies.

A clergy who had thus put themselves into rebellion, for their good old cause, against a Catholic prince, might well hesitate in accepting the present of liberty which was now offered them by their new Protestant sovereign, the King of Holland. Like the cautious High Priest of Troy, who proclaimed his *"fear of the Greeks, and those who were the bearers of gifts;"* so they considered it as a duty to put themselves on their guard against this Protestant protection of the Catholic Church, and narrowly inspect whether mischief might not lurk beneath a Constitution, which was at least suspicious since it bore the name of liberal.

This was a knotty affair; it was an easier enterprise for the allies to overthrow the tyrant of the world, and deliver Europe from its bondage, than for a Protestant prince to render himself popular to a Belgian Catholic clergy.

The English Government was highly interested in supporting the authority of his new Belgian Majesty. It was, in fact, a kind of common concern. The churches of those provinces had been stripped of their principal ornaments, and it was believed that the restoration of the pictures from their bondage, in the Museum of Paris, would be an homage rendered to the faithful and the church, and would, perhaps, soften the opposition of its ministers to the acceptance of liberty.

The public in England seemed at that time to have corresponding sentiments with the government, and to approve the removal of the paintings in sympathy with the Belgic churches. These two causes led the English minister at Paris to give in a note in their favour to the Congress of the four powers who now govern the world, and who were here assembled. The arrival of M. Canova at Paris, at this period, led the English minister to take the same interest for his Holiness the Pope. He represented that the peace of Tolentino could not be the foundation of any right, since the French, after taking the objects in question, had themselves broken the treaty, and that it was therefore just that the more powerful sovereigns should support the cause of the weaker, which was evidently the case with the Pope. Lord Castlereagh furthermore represented the advantages which the arts would obtain by being cultivated at Rome, and that this idea had been so strongly impressed on the French artists themselves, that MM. Quatremere de Quincy, Denon, David, Giraudet, and forty other artists, had signed a petition, before their removal, to the Directory, not to displace those objects.

Those to whom the English minister's observations were known, seemed to consider them as made rather in compliance with a feeling of national jealousy than of strict justice; and, as actions are seldom placed to the account of the principal agents, the ardour of the English cabinet was attributed to the Under Secretary, Mr. Hamilton, a gentleman known in the literary world by his Travels in Greece and Egypt, and highly interested in the progress of the arts.

But however doubtful might have been the right of the French after the treaty of Tolentino had been broken, this reasoning could not be applied to the anterior treaty made with the Prince of Parma, which was the first treaty in which there was any article respecting paintings.

In answer to the note of Lord Castlereagh, a note was given in by M. de Nesselrode on the part of the Emperor Alexander. In this note, the justice or the injustice of the measure was less insisted on than its expediency. It represented the painful situation in which it placed Louis XVIII. with regard to the public; and that if the allies forbore retaking, the last year, what they deemed their property in the Museum, from their respect for the king, this motive ought to operate with double force at the present period.

It was for a short time believed that the Russian note had produced some effect; but whether the Emperor Alexander relaxed in the energy of his representations, or because the Russian troops had withdrawn from the capital, this hope proved delusive.

Further observations were made to the French Government by Lord and some irritation excited at first by the silence which attended them; but still more by a severe note from M. Talleyrand. The dismission of a popular minister at this period had npt, it was said, contributed to increase the cordiality of the Duke of Wellington with the Tuileries.

The war of diplomacy now ceased; sentence was passed upon the Gallery; a decree of retaliation had gone forth, and the attack on the museum began.

The king gave orders to the Directors of the Museum to authenticate whatever violence might be offered. The museum was shut up. It was opened on the requisition of an English colonel, who demanded, with authority, the surrender of the objects which had belonged to the Belgic provinces. English troops were placed on guard at the Louvre. The king ordered tiered the gates to be opened, but that on no pretence any assistance should be given to the invaders.

A kind of Custom-house was established at the gate to examine what should be taken. Sentinels were posted along the Gallery of the museum at every twenty steps, but this did not entirely prevent fraud. The Belgic amateurs, aided by the English soldiery, exercised in alliance their energies. The turn of the Austrians came next, who, though always slow in their operations, never swerve from their purpose. They had appeared to have limited their pretensions to the Horses of Corinth; but, encouraged by the large and liberal example of the Belgians, in taking, they decided on removing the pictures which had come from Parma, such as the St. Jerom of Corregio, those from Milan and Modena, and the Titians from Venice. It was now that the losses of the museum were swelled into magnitude.

The report that a strong guard of foreign troops were posted all night at the Louvre was now repeated from mouth to mouth. The Parisians seemed ready to apostrophize the allies in the same tone of bitter irony with which Achilles addresses Agamemnon in the Iphigenia of Racine:

Un bruit assez étrange est arrivé jusqu'à moi,
Seigneur, je l'ai jugé trop peu digne de foi.

It was sullenly whispered that the allies were going to take away some pictures of the Flemish school. A fearful apprehension, indeed, of something more dreadful, dwelt in every mind; but no one dared to express it. We were in the situation of Madame de Longueville, when she lamented the death of her brother, who had fallen in battle; but dared not inquire for her son. To be bereaved of the Greek *chefs-d'oeuvre*, and of the Italian school, was an idea too full of horror to be borne; a sacrilege from which the. minds of the Parisians started back aghast.

But when the direful truth was promulgated, what language can paint the variety and violence of passion which raged in every Frenchman's breast! Curses, louder and longer than those heaped on the head of Obadiah, were poured out on the allies by the enraged Parisians. They forgot all other miseries; the project of blowing up bridges, pillage, spoliations, massacres, war-taxes, the dismemberment of empire;—all these they wiped away "from their tablets." No longer were their heads plotting on tyranny, on liberty; they thought no more of the cession of fortresses, and the fate of the Constitutional Chart; all principles, feelings, hopes, and fears, were absorbed in this one great and horrible humiliation.

Whatever has been recorded in history of the depredations of the Goths and Vandals seemed light to the public of Paris when weighed in the balance with these outrages of the nineteenth century. They were in vain reminded that these precious objects were the spoils of the vanquished, who had now become the conquerors in their turn; despair seldom reasons. The artists tore their hair, and even the lower classes of the people partook the general indignation. In the liberal access which in this country is accorded to all objects of art and science, the poor had not been excluded. They too had visited these models of perfection, and felt that all had a right to lament the loss of what all had been permitted to enjoy.

It may be observed by the way, that this violence of resentment, this desperate fury at the removal of those master-pieces of art, denote the feelings of a people arrived at a very high degree of civilization. The Parisians, while they had supported with equanimity the most signal calamities, and endured with cheerfulness the most cruel privations, deplored with sensibility, and goaded almost to madness, the loss of objects which, far from being necessary to the wants of ordinary life, are only fitted to charm and embellish its highest state of refinement.

While restitution carried on its labours within the galleries, the four Corinthian horses, once destined to be harnessed to the Chariot of the Sun, placed almost since their birth on triumphal arches, by ancient and modern tyrants; those fiery animals who have pranced from cast to west, and from west to east, as symbols of victory, were now to descend from their gilded car at the entry of the Palace of the Tuileries, in order to proceed on their travels towards St. Mark's church at Venice, where they had been till lately stationed.

It must be observed, in honour of the Austrians, that, in their attempt on the Corinthian steeds, they had at first the moderation to spare the royal feelings at the Tuileries, by making their approaches under cover of the night; perhaps also to avoid wounding the public, as well as the royal eye. There was some delicacy in this proceeding; but the *gardes du corps*, on service at the palace, unsuspicious of such a mark of deference, mistook these Austrian dilettanti for robbers, and charged and drove them from their labours.

The following night, an Austrian piquet summoned to its aid a body of the National Guard. This was a most unwelcome duty to those citizen-soldiers; but as the police of the capital always required their presence in any moment of contention between the foreign troops and the inhabitants of Paris, they were, in the present case, forced to become the unwilling spectators, at least, of this act of national humiliation. Peace was thus preserved; but no progress was made in these mighty operations towards the removal of the horses; and after three nights of ineffectual labour, those animals on the fourth morning still stood on their arch, pawing the air.

But it was now deemed useless to consult feelings of any kind, except those of the claimants of the horses; and the operation of making them descend from their heights was continued in open day. The square was, however, disembarrassed of all French spectators, who were very noisy and troublesome in their disapproval of this spoliation. Piquets of Austrians were placed at every avenue leading to the Place of the Carrousel, to prevent the entrance of any French. The palace and the court of the Tuileries were thus put into a state of siege, of which it was not the king, but the bronze horses, who were the object. Foreigners alone were admitted; and the monarch might have seen from his windows an English engineer exercising his industry to unfetter the animals from their pedestal, the Austrians being clumsy artisans; while English ladies placed themselves triumphantly on the Car of Victory to which the steeds were yet harnessed.

If, in these days of retributive justice, due respect were to be paid to property, those steeds belonged neither to his Austrian majesty nor to the municipality of Venice. In a conversation which passed between M. de Tolstoi, the ambassador from Russia, and Bonaparte, in his days of triumph, on a question respecting the right to the Byzantine dominions, towards which Alexander was suspected to turn his thoughts; it was hinted with some pleasantry by the ambassador, that if Napoleon disputed the pretensions of the Emperor of Russia, it was perhaps in consideration of the claims of Marshal Junot, in right of his wife, who was a Comnene, and really descended from the Paleologues. But in the present circumstances the claims of the House of Comnene, in right of their ancestors, were laid aside, and those of the House of Hapsburg, in favour of the last occupant, the senate of Venice, were admitted.

The horses at length descended from their airy station with safety: not such was the fate of the winged lion of St. Mark's Place at Venice, which surmounted the fountain before the Hôtel of the Invalides. He was now destined to travel the same road with his antique neighbours, the horses of the sun. He had but a small height to descend; his wings outstretched, as if he would have flown to his old perch, or pillar of granite, served him here in no stead, and the operation of his descent was so clumsily performed, that he broke his legs, as well as the edges of the basin of his fountain; while the Parisians felt a vindictive joy at the accident which had befallen him, and which indeed is less to be regretted, as he is an animal of little worth, a whelp only of the middle ages.

While the allied troops were employed in the removal of the Corinthian horses, all the passes to the Place of the Carrousel were guarded by Austrian cavalry, posted at the avenues of the streets that led to it. The Place of the Carrousel was forbidden ground only to the French. Foreigners had liberty to cross it as often as they pleased. I heard an officer call out to an Austrian guard who hesitated, "I am an Englishman, and have a right to pass." The claim was admitted.

The gates the most vigilantly guarded during some days, against the intrusion of the French, were those of the gallery of the Louvre. It was said that this measure was taken from motives of tenderness to those feelings which the scene within must naturally have excited in the French; but it was rumoured also, that exasperation might produce violence, and that the pictures might be defaced, or statues mutilated. The troops of each nation took this post by turns. It was that of the Austrians at my last visit. There they stood, defiance in their eye against all Frenchmen, and fresh green branches stuck in their caps: this is the usual ornament of the Austrian soldiers' hat or cap, when in campaign; but these branches appear so much like symbols of victory, that they are highly offensive to the French. When foreigners required admittance, the doors were thrown open. The Frenchmen who were refused, glanced at the laurelled-cap, bit their lips, muttered imprecations, and withdrew.

Some few had, however, the address to procure entrance; they were but few; I found some artists pacing the Gallery of the Paintings; they had an air of distraction, and were muttering curses "not loud, but deep." "*Que le tonnerre du Ciel!—Oh! ç'en est trop!—ç'en est trop!*"—and other exclamations in the same style. A chill sensation came across my heart when I descended to the Halls of the Sculpture, and saw the vacant pedestal on which had stood "*the statue that enchants the world.*" I gazed on the pedestal; one of the old liveried attendants of the hall, interpreting my looks, said to me, in a sorrowful tone, "*Ah! Madame, she is gone, I shall never see her again!*"

"Gone!" said I.

"Yes, *madame*, she set out this very morning at three o'clock, *et sous bonne escorte*."

The old man seemed to mourn over Venus as if she had been his daughter. The adjoining hall presented a few days after a most melancholy spectacle. There lay the Apollo on the floor, in his coffin. The workmen were busied in preparing him for his journey, by wedging him in his shell; and an artist was tracing his celestial features, when the trowel with its white paste, passed across his divine visage. His arm was still majestically stretched out. The French artists who were present wept over it—they pressed his hand to their lips, and bade him a last *adieu!* The scene was now closed on that perfect image worthy of almost divine honours—He was going to add a new glory to Rome, and draw new pilgrims to his shrine—but to Paris he was lost for ever, and she might well deplore her calamity; she had indeed seized him as her captive, but she had gazed on him with unwearied admiration; she had hailed him as the most splendid trophy of victory; and she would have purchased his stay with her treasures, even with her blood, had not resistance been unavailing.

In the package of these divinities much apprehension was felt of their sustaining some injury. The necessary aid and tools were wanting. No rewards, no menaces, however, could prevail on the French *crocheteurs*, porters, and labourers, plying in the streets for employment, to lend their aid. The French, of the lowest class, were too indignant and mutinous to be the abettors of such spoliation. The ladders of the master of an exhibition of singes *savans*, learned monkeys, in the neighbourhood of the Louvre, were at length put in requisition to unhang the pictures. The Pythian divinity of Olympus lay in the streets all night, and might have suffered from any accidental tumult; and the Venus de Medicis was fated, like an abandoned female, to take up her abode for some hours in a common guard-house.

In taking down the Transfiguration, this invaluable picture, the most perfect that exists, was suffered to fall to the ground. A general shudder from the artists around marked this disaster. The painting is on wood, and so worm-eaten, that in some parts it is not an eighth of an inch thick. The dust from the worm-holes covered the floor round the picture, and excited the most terrible apprehensions. It required some courage to inspect it; happily it was found not damaged.

The commissaries of the Duke of Tuscany, having sent off the Venus, laid their hands on the Madonna della Seggia.

This beautiful production of Raphael is one of the few pictures that have suffered from their residence at Paris; though it is difficult to decide whether this picture was injured, because in Italy it was covered with a glass, and the evaporation of the oil could not freely circulate, or if a *glacis* has been taken off at Paris in cleaning the picture. The seizure of the objects which made part of the price of the treaty of Tolentino, consummated the destruction of the museum, so that there does not remain above a twentieth part of the pictures.

The Spaniards claimed their share in this general distribution, and succeeded better than they had done in their purpose of invasion; of which it appears, that the principal motive was that of obtaining new clothes, since they had heard, with some envy, that almost all the troops of Europe had made their toilette at the expense of France.

In the latter times of Bonaparte, in the year 1814, an exhibition had been made of the subjects of the Spanish school; of the Italian, before the time of Raphael; and of the German school. Some French marshals, to please their master, had sent their Morellos to swell this exhibition; which pieces had, by chance, been left during the reign of the Bourbons, the short invasion of Bonaparte, and to the present period.

The Spanish ambassador would not have demanded the Morellos, had they remained in the houses of those who had taken them; but as he found them collected in an exhibition, he took advantage of the negligence of their fresh owners, and sent them back into Spain.

And lastly presented themselves the commissaries of the King of Sardinia. They came at an unlucky moment. The Austrian guard at the museum had been called away to assist in the removal of the horses at the Tuileries. The guardians of the museum, raised into indignation at the attack of these new commissaries, collected their forces, consisting of numerous workmen, and with brush and broom swept the Sardinians out of the gallery.

An attack meanwhile was directed against the National Library. Among the manuscripts of the Vatican, which was ceded by the peace of Tolentino, were those which had been pillaged from the library of Heidelberg, in the Palatinate, during the Thirty Years war, by the soldiers of General Tilly. These spoils were at that period given to the Pope.

The commissaries of the Margrave of Baden laid violent hands on those manuscripts, as the original property of their master, now sovereign of Heidelberg. These manuscripts, both Greek and Latin, amounted to four thousand, and had been taken from Rome, Venice, and the Ambrosian library at Milan. It would have been happy if all had gone that road, since the Vatican is the grave of manuscripts. Whatever appertains to the sciences and literature is there lost to the world; the arts only may possibly be gainers. On the principle of reclaiming the property of past ages, it would be extremely difficult to make out a regular European inventory.

Madame Junot, being descended from the Paleologues, might, on this enlarged plan of retribution, have put in her claim to the Horses of the Sun. A Belgic commissary had a reclamation to make for the town-clock of Troyes, in Champagne, which had been taken from Cambray in the time of Charles VI. about four hundred years since.

The Duke of Wellington may perhaps be taxed with remissness, for having overlooked, in this hour of retribution, certain property that belonged to England.

When Bonaparte, some years since, was on the point of executing his threatened invasion of England, it was deemed expedient to excite the Parisians to a sympathy with such heroic enterprise. Volumes of the history of fifteen or twenty invasions were circulated; but nobody read or believed them. On the maxim of Horace, that what is seen with the eyes produces much greater effect than what passes through the ear; the walls of the Museum were covered with pictures, proving that the measure was not only possible, but had really been executed.

The history of this marvellous transaction was impressed on Parisian incredulity by the display of Matilda's tapestry, worked by the queen and her ladies of honour, representing, in worsted epic, the heroic feats of her husband, William the Conqueror. Hume, in his History, refers to this tapestry, to authenticate some incident of that period.

The Duke of Wellington, it appears, had made no inquiry after this historical furniture. He had, however, a clearer right to the tapestry than the Belgic commissary to the town-clock of Cambray. The tapestry is evidently the property of the prince regent, as heir-at-law to William the Conqueror, to whom it originally belonged, as the husband of Matilda.

The duke might, however, from a sentiment of generosity, have left it to adorn the now naked walls of the museum, and to console the French that their ancestors had once conquered England and taken London, though it were nearly a thousand years since.

The French, when their days of mourning and humiliation are past, will reflect with some consolation on what they still possess. A respectable gallery may yet be formed, when the subjects are duly collected. The Rubens, the Le Seurs, and the Vernets, now composing the collection of the Luxembourg, may be united with the Poussins, and the Miguards of the Trianon. There are also some Raphaels, that of Francis I. the Holy Family, and the St. Michael; some pieces of Leonardo da Vinci, of Claude Lorrain, of Champagne, and the battles of Le Brun.

The collection of sculpture that remains is unrivalled, except by that of Italy. Lord Elgin's collection is thought to be more precious for the learned artist, on account of the number of mutilated fragments it contains; but can give no pleasure like that produced by the sight of the Apollo, or the Laocoon.

Paris retains the Diana from Versailles, the Pallas de Veletri, which was purchased by Bonaparte; and also the museum of the Prince Borghese, in which shines the Gladiator, and many other subjects which may be compared with the first-rate pieces of the Vatican. Bonaparte had purchased this collection by the cession of estates in Piedmont to his brother-in-law. His Sardinian Majesty, on his arrival in his domains, confiscated this property. Apprehensions were entertained that this measure would occasion the loss of this precious collection; but the Congress of the four great powers who deem themselves invested with the high police of Europe, signified to the King of Sardinia that he must repeal his act of confiscation.

The Paris museum might also have been enriched with the collection which had belonged to Prince Giustiniani, in which were the Michel Angelos of Caravaggio, Guidos, and Carraccis; but this collection has been purchased by the King of Prussia for five hundred thousand *francs*. The collection at Malmaison contained the fine statues of Canova, the Paris, the Psyche, and the Dancing Girl; and some pieces of Claude Lorrain, which Bonaparte had taken from Cassel. The elector had an intention to claim them, but they have been purchased by the Emperor of Russia.

I anticipate all your observations respecting the justice of having stripped the walls of the museum of their treasures. You will tell me that they had been wrested from their rightful owners, that they never could be considered as French property, and that consequently no principle of justice has been violated by their removal. You will add, no doubt, that these *chefs-d'oeuvre* ought to belong to the countries who had the genius to create them, though, at the same time, I presume that you would not wish to send them to modern Corinth, or

Athens. You will have ten thousand things to say on this subject, all equally just and reasonable, but the French are in the paroxysm of despair, when nothing is more irksome than reasoning.

The Parisians assert that, amidst the rapid revolutions of our times, a possession of some years gives as great aright to property as would have been acquired formerly by the lapse of ages. They remark also, with a kind of spiteful sarcasm, that this justice, so vigorously preached, and so severely practised by the allied powers in behalf of statues and pictures, has been less rigidly observed towards human beings; and that while they establish with such grave austerity the rights of inanimate objects, it would have been well, if in the treaties of Genoa, and Venice, and the repartition of souls, the rulers of the globe had never lost sight of the rights of men.

But the most candid among the French have less attacked the justice of the retribution at the museum, than the mode of its execution. Instead of a solemn surrender by formal treaty, to which respect would have been paid, it bore the air of seizing spoils by force, and aggravating the loss by the infliction of useless humiliation.

It may be better for the world that these *chefs-d'oeuvre* of the arts are disseminated. Paris ought not perhaps to be the spot where all were accumulated. There is also an intimate connexion between moveable objects of art and those which are fixed; such as the great monuments of architecture, and the frescos. There exists perhaps a sort of secret sympathy between the Apollo, the Transfiguration, and the Dome of St. Peter's, and the School of Athens.

The French artists reject with horror the accusation that they have tampered in any manner with the paintings, by restoring draperies. No such profanation has taken place. The only use they have made of the pencil has been confined to the replacing in similar colours small spots, not more than the eighth of a line square, where the original colour had scaled off. The artists declare also that these monuments, though assembled at Paris, were always considered as common European property—that they were here in a centrical situation, where all had an equal access to them; that they were more carefully preserved in the museum than in churches, where their position is less favourable to the student; that the smoke of lamps and torches in the Catholic churches is so injurious to the colouring of pictures that a great number of pieces of Julio Romano, of Titian, and even of Raphael were so obscured, that it was only after having been cleaned at Paris that they could be admired in all their parts.

The artists assert, in reply to the observation, that the student feels new energies on the classic ground of Rome, and that Italian skies are more favourable to inspiration than those of northern latitudes—that they have been taught by their own experience, that Paris is a fitter abode for the student than Rome; since, unobserved in Paris, he can fly from crowds to that solitude which is so congenial to genius, and where it can best seek ideal perfection. It may be also observed that, although the morals of Paris may not be pure, they are still less corrupt than those of Rome; a consideration of the highest importance when we reflect on the eternal alliance which exists between the progress of taste and virtue.

Finally, the French artists feel great apprehension respecting the safe conveyance of some of those *chefs-d'oeuvre*, from the haste and want of skill with which they were packed; M. Canova, whom, when announced to a minister as M. *l'Ambassadeur du Pope*, he had pleasantly called M. *l'Emballeur,* not having thought proper, from prudential motives, to attend and act in this latter office. M. Canova has had the precaution to send these monuments of art to Italy, by the Belgic, and the Pillars of Hercules; a circumstance which perhaps gave rise to the calumny that they were destined for Carlton House.

The sacrifice of the museum was now consummated. The Garden of Plants and its cabinet of natural history were destined to undergo a visitation. This Museum contained many objects which had been taken from the Cabinet of Natural History of the Prince of Orange, in the first period of the French Republic.

Restitution was here a more difficult task than at the Louvre. Statues and pictures can easily be identified, and being insulated objects, may be placed without disadvantage in new situations. But in the chain of natural history, the subjects being linked together according to their respective families, the separation of parts becomes a fatal injury to the whole.

The cabinet of the *Stadtholder* was less extensive than has generally been thought. It was not so considerable as that of Paris, and the French commissaries had not taken the whole. In the difficulty of distinguishing this kind of property, the professors of the Garden of Plants proposed an expedient, which was, that of forming a complete duplicate of their magnificent collection for the King of Holland, without distinction of subjects belonging or not to the Stockholder's collection. This proposition was readily accepted by the minister of the King of Holland.

Thus ends the long chapter of restitution. The die is cast, and fears and reasonings, remonstrances and complaints, are alike unavailing. Resentment now beats high in the bosom of the French, but time will exert its accustomed power of softening all impressions. Let us hope that France will learn to bear adversity with magnanimity; and the Allied Powers to use prosperity nobly. They have had much to avenge, but vengeance leads to eternal warfare; and a great nation, driven to despair, might be apt to say with Hamlet, "*I've something in me that's dangerous.*"

Every eye is now fixed on our newly assembled legislature. It was observed at the opening of the session, by a witty statesman, that "there were *deux chambres hautes*, who would talk like *deux chambres basses.*" The truth is, that the House of Commons is chiefly composed of *marquisses*, counts and barons. A member of this chamber boasted that the titled parchments, and badges of nobility of the lower house, far exceed the titles of the house of peers, in which are seated so many senators that were once notorious.

The king will, no doubt, endeavour to reign in the most constitutional manner. He wishes to avoid the shock of parties, and had displayed a remarkable proof of this desire by the nomination of the Duke of Otranto to the ministry of the police. This nomination had tranquillised the patriot party, which is numerous, and even the Jacobin party, which is extremely small. But it irritated the ultra-royalists, those, of whom it has been often said, that they are more royalist than the king, and who wish to bring back France to its state previous to the revolution.

The first ministry was dissolved. The king has composed another, the president of which is known for his wisdom and his moderation.

The debates of the Chambers have already shewn that the government is more liberal than the majority of these representatives of the nation; a strange political phenomenon, and highly honourable to the king. His first solicitude, and that of the two Chambers, will be, no doubt, to establish perfect tranquillity in France. The disorders that have taken place at Nimes, and in the department of the Gard, shew how dangerous it is to suffer the people to exercise sovereign authority. In that province, the Protestants, naturally the most zealous defenders of liberal principles, became the victims of a licentious armed populace, under pretence that they were Bonapartists. This reaction in the south is so much the more to be lamented, that the malignity of faction has sought to injure the royal cause by insinuating that the commissaries of the princes favoured these acts of hostility against the Protestants. It would be an offence to the French government to justify it against such calumnies.

The king, who it appears has a mind superior to the littleness of vengeance, confined to a very small number the list of state-offenders. The ultra-royalists, or what the other factions term les Jacobins *blancs*, call aloud for a general epuration. They seem to think, like the Ultras in the time of our Charles the Second, that they can never find axes and ropes enough to punish the guilty. If the government did not set bounds to such pretensions, a double reaction would take place; one against the friends of civil liberty, who would be exiled as Jacobins, and Bonapartists; and another composed of the patriots, and of all the lower classes of the people, against the nobles. Let us hope that all parties will rally round the king, and the constitutional government.— France would be exposed to great danger if any new disturbances arose. An hundred and fifty thousand foreign troops remain on the territory. The foreign powers would take advantage of such a state of disorder, and perhaps compel France to make territorial sacrifices.

Those who have begun disturbances would pretend that there was a scission among the allies, and that they had at least one of those powers on their side. Credulity will do the rest. The people were made to believe six months since that Austria was about to declare itself in favour of the young Napoleon.

You interrogate me respecting the permanence of peace, as if I could read the book of futurity. Nations demand guarantees for their tranquillity, and those guarantees, by the outrages committed on the rights of national independence, become new causes of war. We might have hoped that the last war, and the peace of Paris, would have extinguished the hatred of the nations of the German race against France. No!—in the north of Germany, and in the west, on the banks of the Rhine, it is said on all sides, that the sovereigns may in vain make peace; that the struggle has been that of nations, and not of dynasties; and that the Germans will never consider the quarrel with France as terminated, till Alsatia and Lorraine, and all the conquests of Louis the Fourteenth, be restored, and united into a kingdom of Burgundy, governed by a German prince.

The governments of Europe have been more moderate than the people; they have not negotiated for provinces, but for fortresses, which the Germans pretend to be points of attack against them. In this negotiation the Emperor Alexander has again displayed that noble and generous character by which he has so long acquired the admiration of the French.

Bonaparte is fallen. There is no probability that France can for a long series of years become dangerous as a warlike nation. The purpose therefore of the alliance of Chaumont no longer exists; but the Congress of Vienna, the personal friendship subsisting between the allied sovereigns, and the habitude which the several cabinets have contracted of transacting affairs together, and of being in perfect intelligence with each other,, may perpetuate the alliance of the four great powers. Politics have assumed new forms. The expressions "*Europe insists—Europe will not permit*"—now signifies that such is the will of the Cabinets of London, Petersburg, Berlin, and Vienna.

In conformity to this diplomatic language, unknown five years since, Spain and France seem no longer to form a part of Europe. This union of the four great powers gives them an immense physical force. Hence the idea of forming the High Police of Europe, that is, of governing the world according tot the interests of those four cabinets. It has been observed, that of all the consequences of the French Revolution, this was the most fatal to the liberty of mankind.

An European congress would be, indeed, a flattering dream; but it may be doubted whether that of Vienna will go down with this brilliant title to posterity. Hitherto absolute governments, for the most part, have deformed the continent of Europe; but should a real European Areopagus exist, it will become essential that constitutions should be framed for all the states of which Europe is composed. Some indications of such happy amelioration already appear. The rulers of the world have, indeed, of late years, been compelled to bear so many outrages from lawless power, that they are, perhaps, almost as weary of despotism as the people. France has made the expiation which those who bend to tyranny deserve. But she will lift again her prostrate head! Her natural tendency is towards prosperity. Her destiny points to happiness. Possessing all the materials of which public welfare is composed, she will learn the secret of using them well and nobly; and abhorring the madness of conquest, will enjoy, in calmer triumph, the riches of her climate, her population, her industry, and her arts. Upon the whole, let us hope that the political convulsions which have devastated Europe, will be succeeded by the blessedness of tranquillity; and that moderation, magnanimity, and, above all, the long profaned, but ever-sacred name of liberty, will become the order of the day of the nineteenth century.

Appendix

No. 1.

As soon as the avowed object of the war, the government of Napoleon and of his brothers, had been overturned, and that the nomination of an Executive Commission had destroyed all plans of a Regency, an embassy was immediately sent to the allied powers, to stop the march of their armies, and gain information of their intentions relative to peace.

The plenipotentiaries were General La Fayette, M. Le Forest, a veteran in diplomacy, and the friend of M. Talleyrand; General Sebastiani; M. D'Argenson, a descendant of one of the most illustrious families of France, and who as administrator had resisted Bonaparte's unjust measures at Antwerp; these four were members of the Assembly of Deputies; M. Pontecoulant, member of the Chamber of Peers of the King, and also of the Imperial Chamber, where he had resisted with great energy the proposal of a regency, and refused Lucien the title of French citizen; and M. Benjamin Constant.

The plenipotentiaries repaired first to the French advanced-posts, to ask of the Duke of Wellington and General Blücher a suspension of hostilities. Blücher, who was the nearest, charged himself with the answer. He demanded not only that the fortified posts, before and around him, should be given up, but that all those of the Ardennes., and in Lorraine, should be evacuated. The plenipotentiaries could not accept these conditions; they wrote to Paris to send other commissaries to the two generals, and, furnished with a passport from General Blücher, they reached, athwart many difficulties and delays, the headquarters of the allied sovereigns at Haguenau. The monarchs, and even their first ministers, were not visible; but Lord Stewart, the English ambassador, Count Capo d'Istria for Russia, Count Walmoden for Austria, General Konesbeck for Prussia, held conferences with them.

The vague observations, and reciprocal accusations which passed on political events, are matters of no importance; whatever might have been the instructions of the French, it appears that their conduct was conformable to the interest which they had to leave no pretext to the allies to continue their march. In the conference, General Sebastiani declared that the only object of the war existed no longer; that Bonaparte, now become a private individual under the care of the government, desired only a passport to go to the United States, or to England; that M. Otto was gone to London to ask this permission; that the brothers of Bonaparte were not of the government; that the name of young Napoleon, detained at Vienna, was so much the less obnoxious to the allies, that a provisionary government had been named, altogether opposed to an imperial regency; that nothing prevented an immediate suspension of arms, or conference for a peace; that nothing had been prejudged respecting affairs or persons; that these questions had not been entered on; that they had come to consult the allies; that the plenipotentiaries had extensive powers; and that if the allies proposed any measures that might surpass them, they would immediately refer to the government. Sebastiani's colleagues adhered to his declaration.

The conduct of the allies seemed to prove that they had a contrary interest, that of availing themselves of the victory of Waterloo, by taking possession of Paris without delay. They declared that the allied powers had mutually engaged not to negotiate separately either for a peace, or a truce; and that the negotiation could not commence at Haguenau, but must be delayed till all the cabinets should meet, which would take place as soon as possible. The plenipotentiaries were treated with great respect, but were accompanied by two Prussian officers; and the road they were obliged to take was so prolonged, that they did not reach Paris till the 5th July, two days after the capitulation was signed. I have been assured by generals, that if MM. de la Fayette and Sebastiani had reached Paris in time to be present at the councils of war on the 2nd, it is possible that an attack on the Prussian Army, which had crossed the Seine, would have taken place on the 3rd.

French commissaries, M. Flausergues, General Andreossy, and some others, were sent to the Duke of Wellington. It appears that the duke, at his headquarters, proposed the re-establishment of Louis XVIII. only as an advice; he added, however, that in case another choice was made, the allies would feel themselves obliged, for their own safety, to make some encroachments on the territory, and keep some strong places on their own account. The allies expressed strongly the wish that Bonaparte should be given up to them. It is said, that on this occasion M. de la Fayette made the following answer to one of the foreign ministers:

> I am astonished that when you make such a demand of the French people, you address yourself, in preference, to a prisoner of Olmutz.

No. 2

Declaration of the Chamber of Representatives.

The troops of the allied powers are about to take possession of the capital.

The Chamber of Representatives will not the less continue to hold its sittings amidst the inhabitants of Paris, where the express will of the people has convoked its mandataries.

But in these weighty circumstances, the Chamber of Representatives owes to itself, to France, to Europe, a declaration of its sentiments and its principles.

The Chamber therefore declares that it makes a solemn appeal to the fidelity and patriotism of the national guard of Paris, charged with the protection of the national representatives. It declares that it relies, with the highest confidence, on the principles of morality, honour, and magnanimity of the allied powers, and on their respect for the independence of the nation, so positively expressed in their manifestoes.

It declares that the government of France, whoever may be the chief, ought to unite the votes of the nation, legally emitted, and so co-operate with other governments, as to become a tie, and guarantee of peace between France and Europe.

It declares that a monarch can offer no real securities, if he do not swear to observe a constitution framed by the national representation, and accepted by the people. Thus every government, which should have no other titles than acclamations and the will of a party, or which should be established by force; any government which would not adopt the national colours, and would not guarantee

The liberty of citizens;
The equality of civil and political rights;
The liberty of the press;
The liberty of worship;
The representative system;

The free consent of levies of men and taxes;

The responsibility of the ministers;

The irrevocability of the sales of national property
of every kind;

The inviolability of property;

The abolition of tithes, of nobility old and new, hereditary
and feudal;

The abolition of all confiscation of property;

The full oblivion of the opinions and political votes emitted
to the present times;

The institution of the Legion of Honour;

The rewards due to the officers and soldiers;

The bounties due to their widows;

The institution of juries;

The permanence of judges;

The payment of the public debt;

would have but an ephemeral existence, and would secure neither the tranquillity of France, nor that of Europe.

That if the principles enumerated in the declaration should be either unacknowledged or violated, the Representatives of the French people, now discharging a sacred duty, protest, in the face of the whole world, against violence and usurpation. They confide the maintenance of the dispositions which they proclaim, to all good Frenchmen, to all generous hearts, to all enlightened minds, to all men jealous of their liberty, and, finally, to future generations!

Signed by the President and Secretaries.

www.ingramcontent.com/pod-product-compliance
Lightning Source LLC
Chambersburg PA
CBHW031854090426
42741CB00005B/490